PRAISE FOR MERE MARRIAGE

"Mere Marriage is a well developed and exceedingly relevant study. I know of no other work that has delved so deeply into correspondences between the Greek Fathers and Wojtyla's Theology of the Body."
—From the foreword by Professor Rocco Buttiglione

"Mere Marriage makes an important contribution to moral theology by demonstrating that John Paul II's understanding of the conjugal act is a development of the Church's teaching in Humanae vitae. Using Newman's seven key indicators of a development of doctrine and insights from Michael Buckley, S.J., it compares Paul VI's Humanae vitae with John Paul II's Theology of the Body to show that the anagogic inferences in the latter lie soundly in the area of theological argument and constitute an authentic development of Church teaching. This book is a welcome contribution to the study of Marriage and Family and would be an excellent resource for courses in Catholic moral theology on the topic."
—Dennis J. Billy, CSsR, Robert F. Leavitt Distinguished Chair in Theology, St. Mary's Seminary and University, Baltimore

"Mere Marriage will speak to many who have been inadequately taught for the last fifty years about what makes marriage sacred. Chronicling the wisdom of Popes Paul VI, John Paul II, and John Henry Newman is providential, as all three are newly canonized saints."
—Mary Ellen Bork

"Dedicated, faithful scholars like Andrew Cannon work diligently behind the scenes to provide solid ground for evangelists. I am very grateful to Dr. Cannon for his important book, Mere Marriage, which demonstrates that Saint John Paul II's Theology of the Body combines theological rigor and continuity with sacred tradition to propose an understanding of conjugal love, grace, sacraments, and Christian Mysteries, commensurate with the needs of the new evangelization."
—Christopher West, ThD, President, Theology of the Body Institute

MERE Marriage

*Sexual Difference and
Christian Doctrine*

Andrew D. Cannon, Ph.D.

ISBN: 978-1-7349-4641-3 (sc)
ISBN: 978-1-7349-4640-6 (hc)
ISBN: 978-1-7349-4642-0 (e)

Library of Congress Control Number: 2020908515

Nihil Obstat: Francis M. de Rosa, V.F.
Censor Deputatis

Imprimatuer: Michael F. Burbidge
Bishop of Arlington
March 10, 2020

The *Nihil Obstat* and *Imprimatuer* are official declaration that a book or pamphlet is free of doctrinal or moral error. There is no implication that those who have granted the *Nihil Obstat* and the *Imprimatuer* agree with the content, opinions or statements expressed therein.

Quotations cited as TOB come from John Paul II, *Man and woman He Created Them: A Theology of the Body*, Translation by Michael Waldstein, Copyright © 2006, 1997 Daughters of Saint Paul, Published by Pauline Books and Media, 50 Saint Paul Avenue, Boston MA 02130. All rights reserved. © Libreria Editrice Vaticana, 2020. Used with permission.

Citations to *Humanae Vitae* refer to: "*Humanae Vitae*" Vatican Press. Last modified July 25 1968. Accessed 2016. http://w2.vatican.va/content/paul-vi/en/encyclicals/documents/hf_p-vi_enc_25071968_humanae-vitae.html © Libreria Editrice Vaticana, 2020. Used with permission.

Unless otherwise indicated, Scripture quotations are from the Revised Standard Version of the Bible—Second Catholic Edition (Ignatius Edition), copyright © 2006 National Council of the Churches of Christ in the United States of America. Used by permission. All rights reserved.

Lulu Publishing Services rev. date: 10/19/2020

To our grandchildren:
Helaina, Deaven, Delaney, Daniel, James, Isabella,
Liam, Quinn, Clare and Carolina

The truth is that only in the mystery of the incarnate Word does the mystery of man take on light. For Adam, the first man, was a figure of Him Who was to come, namely Christ the Lord. Christ, the final Adam, by the revelation of the mystery of the Father and His love, fully reveals man to man himself and makes his supreme calling clear.
—*Gaudium et Spes*, #22

Theology is liberated from its immersion in pagan rationality (Platonic, Aristotelian, Stoic, Secular) by that which liberates all of reality, the Event of the One Sacrifice which "for freedom has made us free." When theologians accept this Event in its unqualified historical primacy, it becomes the prime analogate of their theological metaphysics. These correspond to the conversion of the classic Aristotelian act-potency analysis, or to the more ancient form-matter or binary analysis of classic Platonism. Since these pagan wisdoms are efforts to understand the inhabited world (Kosmos) in terms of necessity, in their uncritical acceptance, respectively, by Thomist and Augustinian theologians, each school supposes all reality to be capable of only a deterministic or "cosmological" intelligibility. This view of intelligibility as provided by "necessary reasons" is entirely inappropriate for a properly theological understanding, which is to say, for that "faith seeking understanding" which must be free with the freedom of the faith, and the freedom of its object, Jesus Christ the Lord. Only this inquiry is theological. When the Eucharistic prime analogate replaces the cosmological prime analogate, the universe finds its meaning in the historicity of our creation and redemption by Christ our head.
—Donald J. Keefe, S.J.

FOREWORD

Mere Marriage is a well developed and exceedingly relevant study. I know of no other work that has delved so deeply into correspondences between the Greek Fathers and Wojtyla's *Theology of the Body*. I completely agree with its observations on Wojtyla's method. The relation between Phenomenology and Metaphysics is like that obtaining in the Medical Sciences between anatomy and physiology. Metaphysics gives us the fundamental structures of the human being seen, in one sense, from the outside. Phenomenology gives us access to the way in which man experiences himself from within. Wojtyła organizes the rich experiential material Phenomenologically in the light of the Metaphysics of potency and act. In one sense Phenomenology and Metaphysics are two different disciplines of the same philosophical science. In *Humanae Vitae* Paul VI tells us the objective truth about anti/conception. St. John Paul II's *Theology of the Body* shows the way in which this truth is experienced from within by the person, so that both examinations, the metaphysical and the phenomenological, converge in a unified knowledge of man.

God has endowed man with two main instinctual drives: survival and sex. He shares these instincts with the superior animals, and they pertain to the order of the flesh. Man, however, must assume them in the personalistic order. He has the task of satisfying them in a way that is compatible with personal dignity. To do so he must transcend the limits of an individuality closed in on itself. He must create communities: the community of the family and the community of the workplace, city and nation. These two communities are pillars of the cosmic cathedral. Original sin has corrupted both pillars: in both sex and in work, other persons can be made an object for the individual's self-gratification, exploited and deprived of their dignity.

Christ redeems human nature, restoring the law of love, that is, of self/giving, to constitute true human communities. The order of nature prepares the order of grace and the order of grace is built up on the pillars already prepared by the order of nature. The two pillars are intrinsically connected with one another. The family is also the first community of work in which we learn the virtues of work and on the other hand the family is the inner finality of work: we work for our families.

The sexual instinct is the most powerful force God has impressed in human flesh to prepare man for communion. Fundamentally, Wojtyla thinks that in the order of nature the sexual instinct constitutes a great prefiguration of communion in the order of grace. It drives man out of the boundaries of his self-awareness and makes him feel that he stands in need of another. When we fall in love the emotional center of our life goes out of ourselves to our beloved, and then to our child. Through the conjunction of male and the female bodies children are born and we take responsibility for them. In falling in love we learn that two can be one. We become a community. In pregnancy, in motherhood, in fatherhood, we learn that three can be one. This is the natural basis for the supernatural sacrament of marriage. When we leave our father and mother to create a new family with our spouse, we do not cease to be the sons or daughters of our parents. We bring our relationship to them in our new family. They become the grandparents of our children and our brothers and sisters become their uncles and aunts. In this way a human community grows. This dynamism, integral to the sacrament of marriage, is the dynamism of the family, of the *ecclesia doméstica*, the domestic church, in which we learn the logic of communion. Here we learn the existential attitudes that constitute the communional personality.

This comprehensive vision of the relation between the natural and the supernatural arose from developments in *Ressourcement* theology, in De

Lubac and in von Balthasar, and is especially pronounced in Balthasar's book *Cosmic Liturgy: The Universe According to Maximus the Confessor*.

These ideas of the new theology were in the air in Cracow thanks mainly to the magazine Znak and Wojtyła belonged to the inner circle of its contributors. It is not by chance that De Lubac was invited to write the preface of the French edition of *Love and Responsibility*. However, I think the main sources for Wojtyla were the young people who were his friends and the objects of his pastoral care, the couples he accompanied to their marriage and in their conjugal life. He learned from these young people's lives and he read books only for help in reading their souls.

Mere Marriage's analysis of patristic and medieval theological anthropology illustrates continuity between John Paul's *Theology of the Body* and sacred tradition. Its chapters on anthropology, natural law, personalism and first philosophy show that philosophical methods applicable to an ontology of person vary from methods that apply to an ontology of being. *Mere Marriage's* rigorous comparison of *Humanae Vitae* and the *Theology of the Body* shows that, nevertheless, both ontologies and methods penetrate reality to arrive at inferences and insights that are helpful to theology. This is how the *Theology of the Body* broadens and deepens *Humanae Vitae's* doctrine. *The* analysis also shows that *Theology of the Body's* development of *Humanae Vitae's* doctrine passes Saint John Henry Newman's tests that are designed to disqualify false doctrinal developments.

The *Theology of the Body* responds to a massive contemporary assault on the body, which John Paul understood to be a massive assault on the vital center of Christian faith and culture. He understood that *Humanae Vitae's* pastoral failure led to faltering Christian practice, faltering faith, and faltering culture. The *Theology of the Body* responds to this civilizational disaster by developing *Humanae Vitae's* prior reference to the unitive and procreative meanings of the conjugal act. The conjugal act is the expression and the realization of the one-flesh union of man and woman in indissoluble marriage. Accordingly, *Mere Marriage* explains how the *Theology of the Body* develops an anagogical understanding of marriage, which means its ultimate spiritual and mystical reality as it relates to the Christian mysteries of the Blessed Trinity, Creation, Redemption and Sanctification. *Mere Marriage* contributes a much needed pedagogy of *Humanae Vitae's* doctrine and of the *Theology of the Body.*

Rocco Buttiglione
Professor, Politician,
-Pope Saint John Paul II's
Intellectual Biographer

Pope Saint John Paul II, Canonized April 27, 2014.
Credit: Photo ©Vatican Media

Pope Saint Paul VI, Canonized October 20, 2018
Credit: Catholic News Service; used with permission.

Saint John Henry Newman, Canonized October 13, 2019
Credit: Photo ©Vatican Media

ACKNOWLEDGMENTS

I have many people to thank for making this project possible, none more than Mary Ellen my spouse of fifty years, extraordinary friend, counselor, mother, grandmother and mother-in-law. I wish to thank my dissertation director Father Dennis Billy, CSsR, for his patience and encouragement; Father Joseph Okech, A.J., for his constant friendship and valuable counsel; Father Brian Johnstone CSsR, for his dedication to assisting me and so many other graduate students; Father Donald Keefe, S.J., for his unflinching scholarship; Michael Waldstein for his encouragement to pursue my thesis topic and his monumental contributions to John Paul II scholarship; Father George Rutler and Mary Ellen Bork for reviewing my manuscript; Christopher West Th.D., and Mary Hanlon for carefully editing my manuscript; plus Father Ignacio De Ribera-Martín, Susan Wessel, Kenneth Schmitz, Joseph Capizzi, Charles Pecknold, Christopher Ruddy, John Grabowski and the many other professors, fellow students and friends who helped crystallize themes in this book. Last and far from least, Rocco Buttiglione for his generous gifts of time and wisdom, for his encouragement to get this book into print and for his guidance to readers in offering a *Foreword* clarifying its contribution to scholarship.

EDITOR'S NOTE

References to *Humanae Vitae* within the text are in the form (HV #), and refer to: *"Humanae Vitae"* Vatican Press. Last modified July 25 1968. Accessed 2016. http://w2.vatican.va/content/paul-vi/en/encyclicals/documents/hf_p-vi_enc_25071968_humanae-vitae.html

References to *The Theology of the Body* within the text are in the form (TOB Talk #, Paragraph #), and refer to the monumental *Man and Woman He Created Them: A Theology of the Body;* Translation, Introduction, and Index by Michael Waldstein. Pauline Books and Media, Boston (2006).

The appendix consists of five questions challenging and answers defending the book's thesis.

Mere Marriage: Sexual Difference and Christian Doctrine first appeared as a doctoral dissertation in theology entitled:

Pope Saint John Paul II's Understanding of the Conjugal Act in the Theology of the Body as a Development of the Doctrine of Humanae Vitae: A New Horizon for Theological Anthropology and the Theology of Marriage.

PREFACE

In his *Theology of the Body* Pope Saint John Paul II taught that the one-flesh union of man and woman bound in indissoluble marriage, meaning the conjugal act, is a sacramental sign of the Blessed Trinity, and the Christian mysteries of creation, redemption and sanctification; that it is the foundation of the sacramental order and the order of grace; that this is the "great mystery" of Ephesians. 5:32, and referred to by Paul's mission: "…to make all men see what is the plan of the mystery hidden for ages in God who created all things." of Ephesians. 3:9.

This was not in my catechism seventy years ago. As I read it, I knew enough philosophy and theology to understand this was new and should be shouted it from the housetops. First, I thought, I better confirm my understanding.

So back to school I went. I told an elder cousin I was pursuing a doctorate in theology and he asked why. I said: "Do you remember years ago when we took religion classes?" He said: "Yes." I said: "I want to hear it all again." He said: "You should've paid attention the first time."

I took courses to confirm what I understood from my reading. I couldn't find professors who shared my view of John Paul's integral vision and its potential as a development of doctrine. "Where did that idea come from?" and "That can't be what the Pope taught." were common reactions. I was told my understanding was too radical, over the top, an innovation, outside the main currents of theology and sacred tradition, and that I was wasting my time. I stayed with it to write and now to publish a doctoral dissertation.

Successful doctoral dissertations involve presenting an original thesis, supporting it with scholarly research and defending it to the satisfaction of a panel of qualified professors. My scholarly research demonstrated that my understanding is precisely what the Pope taught and further that his teaching would not be disqualified as genuine doctrinal development by Saint John Henry Newman's tests of genuine developments of doctrine.

Some developments of doctrine merely sharpen the articulation of a mystery. For example, the medieval formula of transubstantiation to describe the Eucharistic mystery. Others change our whole way of thinking about Christian mysteries in general. This would be true of the early ecumenical council definitions that sharpened our understanding of the Incarnation and the Blessed Trinity. These developments were fundamental. They became the foundation of new and comprehensive understandings of Christianity, and changed history.

Another term for comprehensive understandings of Christian mysteries is a theological synthesis. John Paul's *Theology of the Body* takes theology to the threshold of a new synthesis by proposing a comprehensive theological understanding of man, male and female, that enlarges and assimilates prior theological understandings.

Protagoras famously taught that: "Man is the measure of all things; of the things that are, that they are, of the things that are not, that they are not." Likewise, Alexander Pope mused: "Know then thyself, presume not God to scan, the proper study of mankind is man." The point is that all our knowledge refers to our knowledge of man. What we know about man occupies a privileged position relative to our knowledge as a whole.

Anthropology is the study of man and theological anthropology is the study of man in the light of revelation. The *Theology of the Body* is a work of theological anthropology. It proposes a Christian understanding of what man is. Therefore, it proposes to develop our understanding of Christianity as a whole at its foundation.

John Paul's teaching responds to Paul VI's call for a total vision of man and a deeper theological understanding of the truth of marital love (HV 7). It also responds to the Apostolic Exhortation *Familias Consortio's* appeal for theologians to develop the biblical and personalistic aspects of the doctrine contained in *Humanae Vitae* (TOB 133.2,5-6).

As the *Theology of the Body* clarifies our theological understanding of marital love, it deepens and enriches the intelligibility of all Christian mysteries. It sharpens our understanding of what is meant by man being made in the image of God, our understanding of our human dignity and freedom, and the biblical warrant for equality of the sexes. All these threads and more form a unified catechesis in service to culture. John Paul's justification for this project was his belief in the enormity of its importance: "What is at stake here is an authentically 'humanistic' meaning of the development and progress of human civilization." (TOB 129.2)

When the dragons are slain and the curtain falls on our culture wars, a stronger and more confident Christian faith will emerge victorious, and it is likely to be accompanied by doctrinal development. We already know the outcome of the struggle. We just don't know the details of its unfolding. Once our cultural carnage has spent itself, however, Pope Saints Paul VI, John Paul II and Saint John Henry Newman, all recently canonized, and all of whom entrusted their missions to Our Lady, will be recognized as the dragon slayers of the epic and epoch.

This book is riveted on one idea: that John Paul actually taught the radical thesis stated above. It is focused on the teaching itself and its assimilation as Christian doctrine. It does not speculate on its implications or consequences. Its narrow focus seeks only to make Saint John Paul's teaching better known and recognized as a step forward in the direction of Christian renewal and the evangelization of culture.

Parts I and II address background questions of history, philosophy and theology that are essential to the main argument. However, nonspecialist readers may prefer to begin with Part III and read Parts I and II later. The Appendix has five defense questions that may be a helpful summation.

Andrew D. Cannon Ph.D.
McLean, Virginia
May, 2020

Graduate Theological Foundation

Pope Saint John Paul II's Understanding of the Conjugal
Act in the *Theology of the Body* as a Development of the
Doctrine of *Humanae Vitae*: A New Horizon for Theological
Anthropology and the Theology of Marriage

A Dissertation Submitted in Partial Fulfillment of the
Requirements for the Doctor of Philosophy Degree in Theology

By

Andrew D. Cannon
McLean Virginia

September 21, 2018

CONTENTS

ABSTRACT

Pope Saint John Paul's Understanding of the Conjugal
Act in the *Theology of the Body* as a Development of the
Doctrine of *Humanae Vitae*: A New Horizon for Theological
Anthropology and the Theology of Marriage.

Pope Saint John Paul presented the catechesis known as the *Theology of the Body* beginning on September 5, 1979; approximately eleven years after Pope Paul VI promulgated the encyclical *Humanae Vitae*. John Paul characterized the *Theology of the Body* as an extensive commentary on the doctrine contained in *Humanae Vitae*. The doctrine contained in *Humanae Vitae* is that every conjugal act must remain open to the transmission of life. This thesis proposes that both teachings focus on the conjugal act, and that the *Theology of the Body* develops the doctrine of *Humanae Vitae* by developing the theological understanding of the conjugal act.

Theological anthropology, natural law, personalism, ontology, and the authority of papal pronouncements are introduced as background information. Comparison of *Humanae Vitae* and the *Theology of the Body* identifies commonalities and divergences between the two documents. Further analysis of *Humanae Vitae* and the *Theology of the Body* shows that the conjugal act is central to both teachings and that the *Theology of the Body* deepens and amplifies *Humanae Vitae's* theological understanding of the conjugal act. References to John Paul's essays and works such as

Love and Responsibility, *The Acting Person*, and his Second Vatican Council interventions, lend support to his argument in the *Theology of the Body*.

John Paul's proposal develops the doctrine of *Humanae Vitae*. Doctrinal developments may affect more than the doctrine at hand, and the *Theology of the Body's* proposal affects more than *Humanae Vitae's* moral doctrine. The *Theology of the Body* affects our theological understanding of the Christian mysteries of the Blessed Trinity, creation, redemption and sanctification, the sacramental order and the order of grace.

The potential of John Paul's proposal to be defined as doctrine is analyzed under the guidance of Blessed John Henry Newman's *Essay on the Development of Christian Doctrine*.

All the areas affected by the *Theology of the Body's* proposed development of the doctrine of *Humanae Vitae* are not developed in this study.

No full-length study has focused specifically on *Theology of the Body's* theological understanding of the conjugal act as a development of the doctrine of *Humanae Vitae*.

GENERAL INTRODUCTION

Pope Saint John Paul presented the catechesis known as the *Theology of the Body* to his Wednesday general audiences between September 5, 1979 and November 28, 1984, beginning approximately eleven months into his papacy and eleven years after Pope Paul VI promulgated the encyclical *Humanae Vitae* on July 25, 1968. The subject of *Humanae Vitae* is the conjugal act, and specifically, the morality of contraceptive birth regulation.

Having read the *Theology of the Body*, one talk per day for about five months, I sensed that it was a new, innovative, appealing and important teaching. I thought it shed new light on theology, that it developed doctrine and that it would challenge theologians to assimilate its teaching. I noted that John Paul II characterized the *Theology of the Body* as an extended commentary on the doctrine contained in *Humanae Vitae*. That motivated me to research the thesis that the *Theology of the Body* develops the doctrine of *Humanae Vitae* by developing the theological understanding of the conjugal act.

John Henry Newman described development as: "The process...by which the aspects of an idea are brought into consistency and form..."[1]

---

[1] John Henry Newman, *An Essay on the Development of Christian Doctrine, Notre Dame Series in the Great Books* (Notre Dame IN: University of Notre Dame Press, 1878), p.38.

The idea in this case is the doctrine of *Humanae Vitae*, specifically, that every conjugal act must be open to the transmission of life [2] (HV 11).

Doctrine develops in the context of urgent historical circumstances. An urgent historical circumstance facing the Church of the last century was the problematic reception of the doctrine of *Humanae Vitae*. The *Theology of the Body* develops *Humanae Vitae* by developing the theological understanding of the one-flesh union of man and woman expressed and realized in the conjugal act.

This study focuses on the process by which the *Theology of the Body* brought aspects of *Humanae Vitae's* moral doctrine into consistency and form. Part I is a review of theological anthropology, natural law, personalism, ontology and papal authority. Part II compares *Humanae Vitae* and the *Theology of the Body* as theological treatises. Part III focuses on how the *Theology of the Body* develops the doctrine of *Humanae Vitae*. Part IV introduces Blessed John Henry Newman's work on doctrinal development. It explains his seven tests that disqualify false doctrinal developments. It applies Newman's tests to see if they disqualify the *Theology of the Body* as a genuine development of *Humanae Vitae's* doctrine. Part V, the final part, contains a summary and conclusions.

---

[2] Pope Paul VI, "Humanae Vitae" Vatican Press, last modified July 25 accessed 2016. http://w2.vatican.va/content/paul-vi/en/encyclicals/documents/hf_p-vi_enc_25071968_humanae-vitae.html

ARGUMENT

Humanae Vitae's doctrine is that every conjugal act must be open to the transmission of life. This doctrine was received as a problematic moral norm. Many Catholic theologians dissented from it in theory and many of the laity dissented in practice.

John Paul II recognized the importance and difficulty of resolving the theological controversies surrounding *Humanae Vitae* and noted that Pope Paul VI had raised the possibility of deepening the explanation of the truth about Christian marriage. John Paul responded to Paul VI's prompting with his *Theology of the Body* proposal to bring consistency and form to *Humanae Vitae's* doctrine by developing the theological understanding of the conjugal act.

While *Humanae Vitae* called for a total vision of man (HV 7), it nevertheless presupposed a traditional theological anthropology that traces to Boethius in the sixth century. That theological anthropology characterizes the human person as a rational animal made in the image and likeness of God by virtue of his rational nature, his immortal soul, intellect and free will. The *Theology of the Body* does not dispute this characterization but considers it to be incomplete because it gives no account of the theological significance of the body and sex. Therefore, from the *Theology of the Body's* perspective, a reason for the problematic reception given to *Humanae Vitae* was its inadequate theological anthropology. John Paul sought a fuller anthropological foundation for a theology of marriage and conjugal love. To meet this need he proposed a more complete theological understanding of the person, the body, sex, marriage and the conjugal act. In this way, the *Theology of the Body* responds to *Humanae Vitae's* call for a total vision of man by proposing to complete *Humanae Vitae's* theological anthropology and bring consistency and form to *Humanae Vitae's* doctrine.

John Paul II begins this theological exposition with Christ's response to the Pharisees' inquiry concerning the lawfulness of divorce in which Christ refers them to the beginning, to Genesis, (Mt. 19:3-8). John Paul proceeds to analyze Genesis' accounts of man's original solitude, original union, and original nakedness, to better understand Christ's specific reference to the indissolubility of marriage. What he discovers is a theological anthropology of the human person, and the conjugal act, more adequate to ground a theology of marriage, and the doctrine of *Humanae Vitae*.

The *Theology of the Body* analyzes the mystery of the human person in the context of the mystery of God. Human persons, and specifically the one flesh union of male and female, are analyzed in the context of the Christian mysteries of the Blessed Trinity, creation, redemption, sanctification, grace and the sacraments.

The *Theology of the Body* deepens, amplifies, and develops *Humanae Vitae's* moral imperative by explicating the conjugal act in the context of the Christian mysteries of the Blessed Trinity, creation, redemption and sanctification. It explains revelation's account of the conjugal act in its anagogic dimension, meaning its ultimate spiritual and mystical sense. In doing so, it strengthens *Humanae Vitae's* appeals to the authority of scripture, to the authority of antecedent magisterial teaching, to nature, to philosophical arguments, and to the teaching authority of the magisterium. It develops *Humanae Vitae's* doctrine by teaching that the one flesh union of man and woman, the conjugal act, images the Blessed Trinity, is a primordial sacramental gift to our first parents, is a prophetic sign of Christ's love for the Church, and is therefore prophetic of the whole sacramental economy and the economy of grace, of creation, redemption, and sanctification. It recognizes the one flesh union of man and woman, in the dimension of gift as foundational to human dignity, ethics and culture. Further, recalling Paul's letter to the Ephesians, the *Theology of the Body* teaches that conjugal love is the '*Magnum Mysterium*' of Eph. 5, and '*the plan of the mystery hidden for ages*' of Eph. 3:9.

METHOD

Recognizing that the *Theology of the Body*, a catechesis, and *Humanae Vitae*, an encyclical, are different genres, comparisons are made using methods for analysis of incommensurable treatises. When truths or knowledge are proposed, the study uses a structure for evaluating truth or knowledge claims. When a development of doctrine is considered, the study uses a structure for gauging doctrinal developments. The gauge of doctrinal development will be borrowed from Blessed John Henry Newman's *Essay on the Development of Christian Doctrine*. Other structures are borrowed from Michael Buckley's analyses of theisms and atheisms.[3] The first structure Buckley uses is from Plato's *Seventh Epistle*[4] for understanding the process of obtaining knowledge:

> For each of the things that are, there are three necessary means through which knowledge is acquired. Knowledge itself is a fourth factor. And the fifth...is the thing itself, that which is knowable and true. Of these the first is the name...the second is the definition...the third is the

---

[3] Michael Buckley, S.J., *At the Origins of Modern Athiesm* (New Haven: Yale University Press, 1987), p. 6, 13-25.

[4] Plato, *Timaeus, Critias, Cleitophon, Menexenus, and Epistles, Loeb Classic Library* (London: William Heinemann 1929).

image, the fourth is the knowledge, the fifth, as has been
said, is the thing itself, that which is knowable and true.[5]

This structure allows naming as a means of acquiring knowledge,
defining as a means of acquiring knowledge, and imaging as a means
of acquiring knowledge. Naming as a means of knowledge is more
common in phenomenological epistemologies. Definition as a means
of acquiring knowledge is more common in realist epistemologies.
Imaging as a means of acquiring knowledge is more common in idealist
epistemologies. *Humanae Vitae's* knowledge of the conjugal act is more
realist and the *Theology of the Body's* knowledge of the conjugal act is more
phenomenological and idealist. The thesis regards all these as valid for
obtaining knowledge and for theological argumentation.

Buckley's second structure establishes parameters for the analysis
of inquiries in general.[6] The parameters are consistency, process, form
or mode, and discourse. The first parameter, consistency, asks what is
constant or consistent about the inquiries being compared. The second
parameter is process, which concerns how the constant or consistent
elements are transposed from one treatise to the other. The third
parameter, form or mode, concerns the form or mode of thought that
obtains in each of the disparate treatises. Lastly, the fourth parameter,
discourse, introduces the world of language and literature into the analytic
process. It treats each of the disparate treatises as a literary event that is
therefore open to discourse with the other despite their different processes
and forms or modes of thought. Discourse serves as a neutral instrument
through which both treatises may be interpreted.

Buckley's third structure is used within the discourse parameter of
his second structure.[7] It has four coordinates: selection, interpretation,
method and principle. Buckley explains:

---

[5] Buckley, 6.
[6] Ibid., 13-20.
[7] Ibid., 21-25.

These coordinates allow a series of questions to be leveled at any tractate, speech, argument or discursive expression, and a subsequent relationship to be drawn between one text or inquiry and another, without either reducing every philosophy to a single true philosophy, or regarding all positions as of equal worth because each represents a different perspective. To ask questions governed by these coordinates is to look for the values given to certain variables in every discourse.[8]

Broadly: the selection coordinate concerns what it is that the discourse is about; interpretation concerns what manner of inference can be made according to what evidence, and what form or mode of thought; method "indicates a pattern of discourse, a way of procedure, a manner of argumentation in which one is able to move from one proposition to another."[9] Lastly, principle; "The principle is the source of the discourse, of its truth, its value, or its connection with reality."[10]

These structures help to clarify likenesses and distinguish real or apparent differences between the encyclical and the catechesis and help to refine the elements of both genres into inferences or working propositions to be further analyzed as developments of doctrine under the guidance of Newman's *Essay on the Development of Christian Doctrine*.

---

[8] Ibid., 21.
[9] Ibid., 22.
[10] Ibid.

PART I

Theological Anthropology, Natural Law, Personalism, Ontology, Authority

I. Introduction to Part I

Part I of the dissertation, a preamble, provides background information in five sections. The first section, on theological anthropology, illustrates the vitality and persistence of inquiry into theological anthropology by outlining examples of anthropological proposals from tradition going back to the patristic and scholastic periods. The second section is a contemporary presentation of natural law theory and illustrates the philosophical anthropology undergirding *Humanae Vitae's* moral argument. It analyzes a recent International Theological Commission (ITC), study, *In Search of a Universal Ethic: A New Look at the Natural Law.*[11] The third section presents personalism, and illustrates the anthropological perspective operative in the *Theology of the Body*, which deepens *Humanae Vitae's*

---

[11] Various, *In Search of a Universal Ethic: A New Look at the Natural Law* (The Vatican International Theological Commission, 2009), http://www.vatican.va/ roman_curia/congregations/cfaith/cti_documents/rc_con_cfaith_doc_20090520_ legge-naturale_en.html.

anthropology and creates the space needed to enable further development of its doctrine. The fourth section presents ontology, and contrasts a metaphysics of being and a metaphysics of person in twentieth century ontology. The fifth section presents the different levels of papal authority associated with papal encyclicals and papal catecheses.

I.1 Theological Anthropology

Theology studies God, and anthropology studies man. Theological anthropology studies man in the perspective of revelation which includes sacred scripture, sacred tradition, nature or creation, and the fullness of revelation, -Jesus Christ.

Theological anthropology asks, with the psalmist: "what is man that you are mindful of him?"[12] It seeks to understand the creation narratives of Genesis. There, man and woman are situated at the pinnacle of creation as its heirs and stewards, vested with freedom and with surpassing dignity as the *imago Dei*, the image of God. There, too, through disobedience, man is resituated, banished from paradise, sentenced to toil, yet he retains God's gifts of freedom and the *imago Dei*.

Theologians shape these data into narratives of man's origin, history and destiny. The narratives vary with different theologians who explain the Genesis creation stories in different historical contexts and from different philosophical perspectives. Yet, after two thousand years of Christianity the psalmist's question persists: "what is man that you are mindful of him?" John Paul offers the *Theology of the Body* to answer the psalmist's question in our historical context, in a contemporary philosophical perspective, and in response to the difficulty and importance of questions raised by the encyclical *Humanae Vitae*.

This chapter illustrates the perennial vitality of the psalmist's question. It presents different anthropological proposals by various theologians and

---

[12] *Revised Sandard Version Bible, Ignatius Edition*, Second Catholic Edition ed. (San Francisco: Thomas Nelson Publishing, for Igantius Press, 2006).Ps. 8:4

philosophers representing a great variety of understandings of: God's activity in creating man; man, as the image and the likeness of God, the *imago Dei*; man's spiritual aspect, his spirit, and soul; man's body and sex; redemption and eternal life. They include notions of spiritualized bodies and corporal bodies in the Resurrection. One explains our inclinations to evil as rooted in our bodies that have been corrupted by the Fall, and other explanations root our evil inclinations in our imaginations that have been corrupted by the Fall. We find the logos of Neoplatonism and the Logos as Christ. We discover analogies between the family and the Blessed Trinity understood in different ways by different theologians. We encounter understandings of marriage in relation to Trinitarian theology, Christology and to the Paschal mystery. All these and other understandings have been proposed and this chapter illustrates a few examples.

These profiles of theological anthropology are intended to suggest the wide variety of anthropological proposals reaching back to Christianity's first encounters with Greek and Roman society. They offer a perspective in which to view John Paul's unique proposal as one more in a long-running series of Christian proposals. Moreover, they convey a sense that theological anthropology has remained open to development throughout history.

Each sample of theological anthropology has philosophical and historical dimensions that supply a deeper understanding of their relevance. However, analysis of these dimensions for each of the examples would go beyond the scope of this study. On the other hand, the philosophical and historical dimensions underpinning the anthropologies operative in *Humanae Vitae* and in the *Theology of the Body* will be considered in greater detail.

I.1a Examples of Theological Anthropologies from Tradition

PHILO JUDAEUS (c. 12 BC - c.47 AD)

(Dual Creation; Body, Soul Dualism; man's mind images the logos, -the true image of God)

Philo Judaeus was an influential first century Jewish philosopher and theologian. He understood man as created by God in primarily Platonic, dualistic terms. Man is made up of two components, the material body and the rational soul or mind. Philo understood the two Genesis accounts of the creation of man as a dual creation, one for the mind and the other for the body. In the first account (Gen. 1:26-30), Philo understands that God creates a rational and incorporeal being, a heavenly man. This is the creation of the rational soul or mind of man, which is in the image of God.[13] Philo understands the second account (Gen. 2:7) to mean that God creates man's body and breathes his spirit into his nostrils so that man came into existence, an earthly man, as a body and a soul.[14]

There are two noteworthy characteristics of the *imago Dei* as understood by Philo. The first characteristic is that Philo understands that man, as the *imago Dei*, is an image of an image. Man is in the image of the logos, which is the *imago Dei*. The logos for Philo is posterior to God and is an idea of God by which He creates the universe. The logos both precedes and permeates the universe. The mind of man, then, in relation to his body, models the logos in relation to the universe. The logos is compatible with the Platonic notion of world-soul, and it is the logos that is the *imago Dei*.[15]

The second noteworthy characteristic is that the spirit God breathes into man in the second Genesis account is understood by Philo to be a

---

[13] D. T. Runia, "God and Man in Philo of Alexandria," *Journal of Theological Studies*, no. 39 (April 1988).

[14] Ibid., 69.

[15] Ibid., 67.

part of the logos. Here the image of the logos is understood not in the same sense of the first characteristic, as a *model* of the logos, but as a *part* of the whole of the logos. Philo is content with the idea that man can be an image of the logos as a model in one sense, and a part of the whole of the logos, in another sense.[16]

In Philo's dualist anthropology the body is understood to be corruptible and is not in any way a participant in the divine image, nor in the ultimate divinization of man, both of which concern only the rational soul. To Philo, the rational soul or mind is god to the body. The body is corruptible. The body is also the source of pleasures, which bring man to ruin.

SAINT IRENAEUS OF LYONS (c. 120 – c. 200)

(Adam created in the image of God; only potentially His likeness; Christ is true image and likeness; Christ restored man's potential for likeness; and the Holy Spirit re-incorporates man into Christ)

According to Irenaeus, Adam was given the *imago Dei* at creation along with the potential to develop into the *likeness of God*. Adam forfeited his potential to develop into the *likeness of God* by his disobedience. The true *image and likeness of God* is realized only in the God/man Jesus Christ.[17] Jesus Christ, by his incarnation, death, and resurrection, restored and recapitulated Adam's (and all of his progeny's) potential for achieving the *likeness of God*.

Restoration of the *likeness of God* is accomplished in each one of us by the two hands of God, namely Jesus Christ and the Holy Spirit, who execute the Father's will to fashion each man into *the likeness of God*. The first hand, Jesus Christ, by his incarnation, passion, death,

---

[16] Ibid.

[17] James G. M. Purves, "The Spirit and the Imago Dei: Reviewing the Anthropology of Irenaeus of Lyons," *Paternoster Periodicals* LXVII, no. 2 (April 1996).

and resurrection, redeems, restores, and recapitulates man's potential to achieve the *likeness of God* through transformation and incorporation into Christ. The transformation and incorporation into Christ is the work of God's other hand, the Holy Spirit, the Wisdom of God, who assists man in his development so that the transformation and incorporation into Christ and the *likeness of God* is realized.[18]

Interestingly, Irenaeus does not concern himself much with the *Soul* and places emphasis on the *Body* as the image of Jesus Christ the incarnate Son. Arguing against Gnosticism, Irenaeus stressed that an image must have a form and a form can exist only in matter. Consequently, he is emphatic that the image of God in man is described quite concretely in the flesh. "An image also has a revelatory function: the image reveals the archetype of which it is an image."[19]

For Irenaeus all Christian mysteries, the *imago Dei*, the Blessed Trinity, the Incarnation, the Paschal Mystery, the Resurrection, the gift of the Holy Spirit, are understood as a whole cloth, soteriologically. For Irenaeus all Christian mysteries are denominated in terms of the salvation of each man, and all men, who as heirs and sharers in the humanity of Adam, become heirs and sharers in the divinity of Jesus Christ.

ORIGEN (c. 185 - c. 255)

(Dual creation; Christ is imago Dei; man is an image of the image, not likeness; man can transform himself into likeness by focusing on Christ; Origen offers options for the constitution of the soul and bodily glorification)

Origen like Philo understood the two Genesis accounts of creation as a dual creation. In Gen 1:26, God *made* "...our inner man, [which

---

[18] Ibid., 111 ff.
[19] John Behr, *Asceticism and Anthropology in Irenaeus and Clement* (Oxford: Oxford University Press, 2000), 89.

is] invisible, incorporeal, incorruptible and immortal."[20] In Gen. 2:7, God *formed* our body: "For the text says 'And God formed man,' that is fashioned, 'from the slime of the earth.'"[21] Origen, like Philo, considers the *imago Dei* in man, to be an image of an image. It is Christ who is the *imago Dei* and man is in the image of Christ. Origen exploits the distinction between *made* in the first account, and *formed* in the second account, to demonstrate that the body does not participate in the *imago Dei*. Origen is emphatic that it is the inner man of the first creation that is made according to the *imago Dei*. To anyone who would think of the man of the second creation, the man of flesh, as being in the *imago Dei*, he says: "It is most impious to think this about God."[22] His attitude toward the body borders on contempt when compared to his understanding of the inner man whose distinctiveness is indicated by the fact that: "Only heaven and earth, the sun, moon, and stars, and now man have been *made by God*, but all the rest is said to be *made by his command*."[23]

In addition to a dual creation, Origen distinguishes the *image* and the *likeness* in Gen. 1:26. The image is given in this first creation. Throughout life this image can be marred and come to more closely resemble the evil one. By focusing throughout their lives on the *imago Dei*, who is Christ, men can transform themselves into his likeness.[24] Origen sees the task of transformation as achievable through man's efforts, according to his ability and diligence in education.[25]

Lastly, Origen understands man as composed of body, soul and spirit. However, he offers his readers a menu of options concerning the soul. The first option is that man has two souls, a lower soul, and one that

---

[20] Origen, *Homilies on Genesis and Exodus*, *The Fathers of the Church: A New Translation* (Catholic University of America Press, 1982).

[21] Ibid., 63.

[22] Ibid.

[23] Ibid., 62.

[24] Ibid., 65.

[25] Arne J. Hobbel, "The Imago Dei in the Writings of Origen," *Studia Patristica* 21 (1989).

looks heavenward. Option two is that we have one soul and that it is our *bodies* that incline us to evil. Option three is that we have one soul with three parts, a rational part and two irrational parts: one for appetite and one for passion. Origen dismisses option three as an invention of Greek philosophers that "…I do not believe to be strongly confirmed by the authority of divine scripture, whereas for the other two a certain number of passages may be found in the divine writings which appear capable of being applied to them."[26] He then discusses the other options and allows the reader to choose "which of them deserves the preference."[27] Similarly, he concludes his third book on the *Ascent of Souls* by leaving it to the reader to decide whether at the end of time the Son will hand us over to the Father in our bodily nature or as he would have it, as a spiritualized body.[28]

SAINT GREGORY OF NYSSA (unknown – c. 278)

(Creation happened all at once; man is image and likeness of God, but image excludes the body; sex, procreation and mortality given as a remedy after the Fall; risen bodies will be spiritualized)

In *De Hominis Opificio*, On the Making of Man, Gregory of Nyssa celebrates the *Body* in great detail as good and excellent.[29] As an instrument of the immortal rational spirit, the *Body* is integral to man's mastery and majesty over all creation.[30] Moreover, Gregory understands that the image and the likeness to God are both given to man at creation. However, in

---

[26] Origen, *Origen on First Principles* [De Principiis], trans. G. W. Butterworth (Gloucester: Peter Smith 1973).

[27] Ibid., 236.

[28] Ibid., 255.

[29] Gregory of Nyssa, "On the Making of Man," (2005), http://www.ccel.org/ccel/schaff/npnf205.pdf.

[30] Ibid., IV.

Gregory's understanding, our mortal bodies do not participate in the *imago Dei*.

Gregory construed the creation of man to be a single all-encompassing act in which God created all of mankind, the whole human race, in his image and likeness.[31] In addition, foreseeing that man would use his free will to sin, God made man, male and female.[32] Gregory employs the idea of a double creation in a different way from Philo Judaeus or Origen. For example, Philo understood Genesis 1:26-30, as an account of the creation of incorporeal man, and Genesis 2:7 as an account of the creation of corporeal man. Gregory, understanding creation of all men to be a single act, considers Genesis 1:27 "male and female he created them" to be the point at which all mortal bodies were created. Sexual differentiation and death, according to Gregory, were part of creation because God foresaw that after the fall "...mortality and sexuality would have a remedial function...." [33] Furthermore, Gregory understood that "...the creational body was bisexual, while the resurrected body will be neither male nor female"[34] Moreover, the body we have on earth will undergo spiritualization at our resurrection.

SAINT ATHANASIUS (296 – 373)

(Matter, the body, and marriage are all created by God and hence good; Adam's fall corrupted our imaginations, causing sin; the body witnesses to God; divinization includes the body)

Athanasius taught that matter and the human body are not evil, but good. He taught that creation was accomplished by the hand of God and was,

---

[31] Ibid., XVI.

[32] Ibid., XVII.

[33] Gerhart B. Ladner, "The Philosophical Anthropology of Gregory of Nyssa," *Dumbarton Oaks Papers* 12 (1958).

[34] Ibid, 90

therefore, good. Evil on the other hand is not created by the hand of God and in fact has no being or existence of its own. Rather, evil consists in a false imagination in the thoughts of men. It is the mind, not the *Body* that is deceived. This false imagination deceives the free will of man, which moves the members of the body in a way that is opposite to the good. In this way, evil is a contrary use, or a privation, or excess, or an abuse of the good, which is the thing that enjoys true existence.

For Athanasius, the human body, being created by the hand of God, is sanctified and capable of participating in divine nature *-theosis*. Through the *Body* every person can, in his or her social setting, bear witness to God.

On the subject of marriage, Athanasius teaches that marriage is a direct creation of God and is therefore sanctified. Marriage as a union of man and wife that is created by God is good in itself. This contrasts with Augustine's understanding that the good of marriage is derived from its effects. No, to Athanasius, marriage is sanctified and even the Fall did not pervert marriage itself. Rather, the fall deprived Adam and Eve of a heretofore accessible knowledge of God that had enabled them to be self-sacrificial and enabled them to be absorbed not in themselves but in each other. So, the Fall, Athanasius taught, affected the will of man rather than marriage or the body, and hence, marriage is a blessing and a good in itself that even the fall did not take away.

Concerning redemption and marriage, Athanasius taught that God did not scrap the old design. Rather, by redeeming and incorporating man into his own body Christ created man anew and marriage, the peak of God's original plan for the first man, was fully restored. Athanasius saw in the family an icon of the Church.[35] Moreover, he taught sexual relations were God's order implanted in the nature of living creatures as a sign of God's wisdom and goodness.[36]

---

[35] Mathias F. Wahba, *Honorable Marriage According to Saint Athanasius* (Minneapolis MN: Light and Life Publishing, 1996).

[36] Ibid., 186.

GREGORY NANZIANZUS (329 – 390)

(Likens Father, Son and Holy Spirit to human generation, father, mother and child as equal in substance but differing in origination or mode of being)

Gregory Nanzianzus is among the first theologians to structure the family analogy to illuminate Trinitarian theology.[37] In arguing for the consubstantiality of the Trinity, Gregory described the discrete relations among Father, Son and Holy Spirit as modes of existence: Father, as un-generate, un-begotten; Son, as generate, begotten; and, Holy Spirit, as proceeding or taken from. He distinguishes these modes of being from substance which is the same for the three distinct modes of being. He uses a family analogy to clarify these distinctions, specifically Adam, Seth and Eve, representing Father, Son and Holy Spirit, respectively. He asserts that Adam, Seth and Eve, as human beings, are of the same substance, and their distinct modes of being illustrate the discrete relations in the Blessed Trinity. He proposes the following structure of origins to illustrate their modes of being: Adam as Father, un-generate, un-begotten, molded by God; Eve, as Holy Spirit, a portion of the molded creation, taken from Adam, un-generate; and Seth, as Son, generate, offspring of the pair. Gregory understood analogies to serve truth only within boundaries and that they cannot be stretched indefinitely in all directions. With this analogy he sought to illustrate that the common substance of the first family, their humanity, had three different modes of origin. He is not so much intent on illustrating a strict correspondence in modes of being between the first family and the Trinity. His major point was to illustrate that modes of being or origination do not define substance.[38]

---

[37] Lionel Gendron, *Mystery of the Trinity and Familial Symbolism: An Historical Approach* (Rome: Pontifica Universitas Gregoriana, 1975), 33,ff.
[38] Ibid.

SAINT AUGUSTINE (354 – 430)

(Rejects family analogies to the Blessed Trinity; accepts image and likeness to God though he emphasizes dissimilarity; marriage is instrumentally good; marital acts are morally problematic)

Augustine did not envision a two-stage creation, and understood that both the image and the likeness of God were given to man at creation. For Augustine, man is not the image of God in any sense of equivalency. "The term image implies at the same time both similarity and dissimilarity"[39] Rather he is the image of God in likeness according to a hierarchy of likeness in which all creation participates. Man occupies an exalted position in the hierarchy of creation by virtue of the soul's immateriality and power to know the truth. Augustine sees the image of the Trinitarian God in virtually all of creation, but especially in man, notably by virtue of his three powers of being, knowing and loving.[40] Interestingly, in *De Trinitate,* Augustine argues pointedly against the idea that the Trinitarian God is imaged in the human family by spouses and their offspring.[41]

St. Augustine's goodness of marriage is positive and affirming, but marginally so. In polemical engagement with Manicheans, he argues that marriage is good *a priori* because God created it, and it is good *a posteriori* because of the three goods of marriage: offspring, fidelity, and sacrament. Sacrament is understood as a persevering commitment rather than a sacrament of the Church.[42] He upholds the goodness of marriage in an instrumental sense, meaning that marriage is not so much a good in itself. Rather its goodness derives from its effects or what it produces –namely,

---

[39] Johannes Bavel O.S.A., "The Anthropology of Augustine," *Études Augustiniennes* no. 19 (1973): 43.

[40] Ibid.

[41] Saint Augustine, *The Trinity,* trans. Stephen McKenna CSSR, *The Fathers of the Church* (Washington DC: Catholic University of America Press, 1963).

[42] Bavel O.S.A.

offspring, a remedy for concupiscence, persevering commitment, and social friendship.

While he defends the goodness of marriage against the assault of the Manicheans, he seems to be very close to their understanding of the conjugal act. In Augustine's theology, the conjugal act is only sinless when it is engaged in for the purpose of conception and the pleasure derived is only related to the joy of conceiving, and not to the enjoyment of the sensual excitement. It is also sinless on the part of one spouse when it is engaged in to make good on the marital debt or obligation provided that no consent is given to carnal pleasure in the act. Any other use of marital intercourse is at least a venial sin.[43]

JOHN CHRYSOSTOM (c. 347- 407)

(The family images the Blessed Trinity; the Eucharist is a one-flesh union with Christ; Christ took our nature so we could take his; these spousal images celebrate the holiness of marriage)

Saint John Chrysostom, Bishop and Doctor of the Church was ordained Bishop of Constantinople on February 26, 398. Of Chrysostom, Theodore Mackin S.J. has written that:

> Chrysostom's was not a speculative mind, nor was he involved in his lifetime in great dogmatic controversies. Nevertheless, it would be a mistake to underrate the great theological treasures hidden in his writings. From the very first he was considered by the Greeks and Latins as a most important witness to the Faith.[44]

---

[43] Theodore Mackin S.J., *What Is Marriage* (New York: Paulist Press, 1982). 130.
[44] Various, *Catholic Encyclopedia, Patristic Series* (New Advent, 1910), http://www.newadvent.org/cathen/08452b.htm

His contributions to theological anthropology and in particular his theological understanding of Christian marriage, comes to us through his homilies which are unexcelled and highly relevant to the central themes of the *Theology of the Body*.

In his homily #20, on Ephesians 5:22-33,[45] he extends the one flesh union of man and wife, to the begetting of a child, resulting in a three in one flesh allusion to the Blessed Trinity. He adds Christological and Eucharistic dimensions to marriage explaining that Christ took our nature so that we could take his, and that we are one flesh with him in the Eucharist more than our children are one flesh with us.[46] In the same homily he likens the one body of man and wife to the oneness of Christ with the Father.[47] He emphasizes that in Ephesians Paul is not talking about a spiritual reality but a bodily reality.[48] Moreover, he lauds the holiness of marriage as comparable to the holiest of consecrated monks.[49]

In his homily #12, on Colossians 4:18, he comments on the mystery of marriage as the *imago Dei*,[50] and elaborates further the Trinitarian

---

[45] John Chrysostom, *On Marriage and Family Life*, trans. Cathrine P. Roth & David Anderson, *Popular Patristic Series* (Crestwood, NY: St. Valdimir's Seminary Press, 2003).

[46] Ibid., 51. "The Son of God shares our nature so we can share his; as he has us in him, so we have him in us… Paul shows us that a man leaves his parents, who gave him life, and is joined to his wife, and that one flesh – father, mother and child – results from the comingling of the two. The child is born from the union of their seed so the three are one flesh. Our relationship to Christ is the same; we become one flesh with him through communion more truly one with him than our children are one with us because this has been his plan from the beginning."

[47] Ibid., 52. "I say that husband and wife are one body in the same way as Christ and the father are one."

[48] Ibid., 56. He does not say "one spirit" or "one soul" (union like this is possible for anyone), but he says "one flesh."

[49] Ibid., 61-2. "If your marriage is like this, your perfection will rival the holiest of monks."

[50] Ibid., 75. "How is marriage a mystery? The two have become one. This is not an empty symbol. They have not become the image of anything on earth, but of

dimension of three in one flesh.[51] Chrysostom taught that if no child is begotten, there is no diminution of the one flesh union of man and wife.[52]

In a sermon on 'Marriage,' Chrysostom speaks to the purpose of marriage as twofold: to make us chaste, and to make us parents. Of the two, Chrysostom saw Chastity as the primary purpose of marriage.[53] And, in a sermon: on 'How to Choose a Wife,' Chrysostom attributes the love and joy of marriage to the goodness of God.[54]

These homilies on marriage show that John Chrysostom's theological statements concerning the one flesh union of man and woman, the conjugal act, are explicitly Trinitarian, Christological and Eucharistic. He celebrates both the goodness of marriage and its mystical or sacramental dimensions without equivocation.

MAXIMUS THE CONFESSOR (c. 580 – 662)

(Christ is the imago Dei; man images Christ; death, sexual difference, were consequent upon the fall; Man is a microcosm of creation; Christ's recapitulation will eliminate sexual difference)

God Himself."

[51] Ibid., 76. "How do they become one flesh? As if she were gold receiving the purest of gold, the woman receives the man's seed with rich pleasure, and within her it is nourished, cherished and refined. It is mingled with her own substance and she returns it as a child. The child is a bridge connecting mother and father, so the three become one flesh…that bridge is formed by the substance of each!"

[52] Ibid. "But suppose there is no child; do they then remain two and not one? No, their intercourse effects the joining of their bodies, and they are made one, just as when perfume is mixed with ointment."

[53] Ibid., 85. "These are the two purposes for which marriage was instituted: to make us chaste and to make us parents. Of these two the reason of chastity takes precedence."

[54] Ibid., 95. "It is God who sows these loves in men and women. He causes both those who give in marriage and those who are married to do this with joy."

Maximus the Confessor, reminiscent of Irenaeus, presents a whole cloth understanding of the *imago Dei*, the body, Christology, Cosmology and Eschatology. Where Irenaeus focused on the work of the two hands of God the Father in effecting salvation, Maximus is focused on man, the Cosmos, Christ, and the end-times, soteriologically, in terms of Christ's recapitulation and returning of creation to the Father.

According to Maximus there are five divisions or stages of being: 1) created and uncreated; 2) what is perceived by our senses and that which is perceived by our mind; 3) the heavens and the earth; 4) the inhabited world and paradise; and 5) male and female.[55] Man is a microcosm of all creation and the median point between the extremes of all five divisions of being.[56] Christ, by assuming human nature and suffering a death that was unjust and undeserved for lack of participation in Adam's sin, succeeded in conquering death for mankind. Hence, Christ gathers all of the extremes of the five divisions of being into a unity, without annihilation, stage by stage and presents the unity of the Cosmos to the Father. "Thus, he divinely capitulates the universe in himself, showing that the whole creation exists as one."[57]

As for the *imago Dei*, the body and sex, "Man created in the image of God is thus, according to Maximus, a key to understanding creation, not only that he may understand it as it is, but also that by actively understanding it in his process of divinization he may elevate it to the supreme level of its full stereological comprehension."[58] Concerning the body and sex, according to Maximus, procreation through union of sexually differentiated male and female was God's second choice as a means of creating additional human beings. Sex, pleasure and death were consequences of Adam's fall. Accordingly, the first stage of Christ's

---

[55] Andrew Louth, *Maximus the Confessor*, The Early Church Fathers (London: Routledge, 1966), 157, ff.

[56] Lars Thunberg, *Man and the Cosmos: The Vision of Saint Maximus the Confessor* (Crestwood NY: St. Valdimir's Seminary Press, 1985), 73, ff.

[57] Louth, 160.

[58] Thunberg.

unification is accomplished by sundering the division between male and female so that there remain simple human beings, not sexually differentiated, and thus more perfectly deified and integrated into Christ, the true image of God of whom we are an image. In this way those who are faithful to their Baptism are conformed and united to Christ. Through successive stages Christ incorporates the remaining stages of division, uniting all to himself, and ultimately presents the united creation to the Father. "…and thus he fulfills the great purpose of God the Father, to recapitulate everything both in heaven and earth in himself (Eph. 1:10) in whom everything has been created (Col. 1:16)."[59]

RICHARD OF SAINT VICTOR (unknown - 1173)

(Identifies oneness of God with essence and three-ness of God with existence; identifies personhood existentially as unique, relative and incommunicable; advances personalism)

Richard, a Scottish monk, joined the monastery of St. Victor's near Paris between 1120 and 1135. He became Prior of the Abbey in 1162 and died in 1173. Richard's contribution to theological anthropology derives from his treatise on the Blessed Trinity, *De Trinitatae*, published in six books of twenty-five chapters each. His most influential dogmatic work, *De Trinitatae* offers formulae and proofs for the oneness of God and the three-ness of divine Persons in God. With great care he expanded upon the three-ness of God in a way that deepened Christian theology with insights into the dynamism between personhood and substantial being. Not satisfied with the Boethian characterization of human persons as 'individual substances of a rational nature,' Richard broke the concept of 'being' down etymologically and discovered its proper function when it is applied to substances, essences or natures, and when it is applied to persons.

---

[59] Louth.

When the concept of being is applied to substances, according to Richard's analysis, it has the function of identifying a substance or nature that *'is'*. In this usage it is proper to say that God is. There is no intimation of anything other than the super-substantial unitary being of God in this rendering. That is an example of how the concept of being applies to substances. We might also say that man *is*. Both illustrate the being of a substance.

However, that is not our normal way of speaking and not the way we attribute being to substances in common language. Instead we say that God exists or man exists. According to Richard's understanding, to say God exists, while perfectly acceptable in common usage, does not technically have the same fidelity to dogmatic truth as saying that God *is*.

The reason for this, Richard explains, is that the term *'exist'* derives its meaning from a compound word in its original Latin. The term *exsistere* consists of: *sistare*, meaning the nature, essence or substance; and the prefix *ex*, meaning the source, origin, or means of obtaining the nature, essence or substance. According to Richard: "Consequently, with this single verb *exsistere*—or with the single noun *'existence'*—we can intend both that which has to do with the object's nature and that which refers to its own origin."[60]

According to Richard's explanation the Blessed Trinity is One substantial being, existing in three Persons, each of Whom have the same One substantial being, and Who differ only in origin. In this understanding the term person belongs to the category of existence rather than the category of essence, nature, or substance. Each Person in the Blessed Trinity has an identity whereby the substance is One and the same, but the origin is not the same for any of them. In common language, the term existence normally denotes both substance and origin. However, to understand the term person as existential, that is, belonging to the category of existence, rather than essential, and belonging to a category of

---

[60] Richard of St. Victor *On the Trinity*, trans. Ruben Angelici (Eugene, OR: Cascade Books, 2011).Book IV, Sections XI-XII

substance or nature, is to understand important theological dynamics that are also important anthropologically. The characteristics of existential origin account for uniqueness, relativity, and incommunicability. These existential characteristics, in turn, enrich our understanding of the term person and the concept behind it.

Richard's definition of the term person reflects this deeper understanding of the concept. According to Ratzinger, "…he defined person as *spiritualis naturae incommunicabilis existensia*, or the incommunicably proper existence of spiritual nature. This definition correctly sees that in its theological meaning 'person' does not lie on the level of essence, but of existence."[61]

SAINT BONAVENTURE (1221 – 1274)

(Sanctifying grace makes us the imago Dei; Adam rejected sanctifying grace; Sanctification is God's espousal of man; marriage is therefore the sacrament of the union between God and man)

Bonaventure understood creation to be a gift of God to man. He understood man made in the image of God to be the first expression of human life in original justice. This means that God created man in a state of nature in which man was upright and enjoyed the grace of immortality, infused knowledge, and the absence of concupiscence. This is the grace of creation which is completely gratuitous.

Sanctifying grace, on the other hand, Bonaventure understood as grace which makes us pleasing to God and makes us into God's similitude or likeness. In Bonaventure's understanding this grace is not completely gratuitous. That is because he thought that the exercise of our freedom to consent to receive sanctifying grace was a prerequisite to receiving sanctifying grace. Bonaventure understood sanctification, and sanctifying

---

[61] Joseph Ratzinger, "Retrieving the Tradition: Concerning the Notion of Person in Theology," *Communio: International Catholic Review*, no. 3 Fall (1990): 449.

grace to require our consent because he understood sanctification to be a communion of persons, a spousal relationship between God and the man, and there can be no spousal relationship without free consent. In other words, Bonaventure understood the nature of sanctifying grace to be nuptial.

Bonaventure understood the fall in terms of God having offered the gift of sanctifying grace to Adam, which gift Adam was predisposed to receive because he possessed the grace of original justice from creation, but Adam remained free to accept or reject it. Adam rejected sanctifying grace and in so doing rejected God's ultimate gift of spousal union.[62]

However, as Paula Jean Miller points out: "Since the Council of Trent declared that our cooperation depends on God's free gift of sanctifying grace...later theologians did not pursue Bonaventure's approach to the relation of nature and grace in the state of original justice."[63]

Nevertheless, it is noteworthy that Bonaventure's whole understanding of eschatology, our return to God from whence we came, is framed by his understanding of matrimony, the spousal or nuptial union of man and woman, as a sacrament of the nuptial union of man and God in heaven. Like Maximus the Confessor, Bonaventure understands man to be the midpoint or medium of all creation and that his sanctification by Christ represents sanctification of all creation so that all creation is returned to the Father at the end of time.

THOMAS AQUINAS (1225 – 1274)

(Agrees with Augustine's rejection of the family analogy to the Blessed Trinity; but offers an analysis based upon a different trinitarian model, a different rationale, and different grounds for rejection; but is open to reconsideration)

---

[62] Paula Jean Miller, *Marriage: The Sacrament of Divine-Human Communion*, vol. One: A Commentary on St. Bonaventure's Breviloquium (Quincy, IL: Franciscan Press, 1996), 40 ff.
[63] Ibid., 42.

Thomas agrees with Augustine's conclusion to reject the family analogy of the Blessed Trinity. However, to conclude that Aquinas and Augustine were of one mind on the subject is false and misleading. Their analyses differ: first, they frame the analogy differently; second, their theories of knowledge are different; third, they give different reasons for rejecting the analogy; and, fourth, Augustine dismisses the question and Aquinas leaves the question open for reconsideration.

Augustine and Aquinas frame the analogy differently. In Augustine's model Father, Son and Holy Spirit were represented by father, son and mother respectively.[64] In Thomas' model they are represented by the father, mother and son respectively. Augustine's model considered the mother to represent the Holy Spirit, which to Augustine was an absurdity that lacked any intelligible correspondence to the Blessed Trinity. Aquinas constructs the analogy so that the wife and mother correspond to Christ. Thomas describes his model in the *Summa Theologica* as follows:

> The Holy Spirit proceeds immediately from the Father in that he has the being of the Father, and mediately in that he has it from the son: there you have the sense in which one says that he proceeds from the Father through the Son. It is thus that Abel proceeded immediately from Adam, since Adam was his father, and mediately [from Eve], since Eve was his mother and proceeded from Adam. But in truth, this example borrowed from a material origin seems to be a very poor choice to represent the immaterial procession of the Divine Persons.[65]

In this model Christ is represented by the mother. This comports with the Genesis account of Eve's creation from the side of Adam as a figure

---

[64] Augustine, 218.

[65] Thomas Saint Aquinas, *Summa Theologica*, trans. Fathers of the English Dominican Provence, Complete English Edition ed., vol. 1, 5 vols. (Westminster, MD: Christian Classics 1981).ST, I.36.3.1

of the Son begotten of the Father. It further comports with Thomas' Trinitarian theology in that it agrees as to: the number of persons, three; the number of processions, two; and the number of relations, four;[66] in both the family model and in the Blessed Trinity. In this understanding the child, representing the Holy Spirit, has both an active and passive relation to his father and mother, as does the Holy Spirit to the Father and the Son in Thomas' understanding of the Blessed Trinity.

Augustine and Aquinas also differ in their theories of knowledge. Augustine, an idealist, construes knowledge of finite objects in terms of their correspondence with eternal forms. Aquinas, a realist, construes knowledge as adequation of the intellect's representation of real objects to the real objects themselves.

Augustine rejects the analogy because it is 'unseemly'. Aquinas rejects the analogy because it is 'unnecessary'. Aquinas sees only a trace of similarity and considers an analog of a material origin to be a poor choice to represent the immaterial procession of the Divine Persons. Aquinas sidelines the question, commenting that it is unnecessary to pursue the analogy beyond Augustine's conclusion. "Wherefore there is no need to consider the image of God as existing in every part of man."[67]

In other words, Aquinas did not consider the family analogy to the Trinity fruitful for addressing any major theological problem of his day. This implies, however, that a future theologian would be welcome to reconsider the idea if it did address a major theological problem. Alasdair MacIntyre reminds us that: "when Aquinas reached his conclusion, the method always leaves open the possibility of a return to the question with some new argument."[68] Developing the analogy might become

---

[66] Ibid.ST, I.28

[67] Thomas Saint Aquinas, *Summa Theologica*, trans. Fathers of the English Dominican Province, 2nd ed., vol. I (London: Burns Oates & Washbourne Ltd., 1922).(ST, I.93.6.1)

[68] Alasdair MacIntyre, *Three Rival Versions of Moral Enquiry: Encyclopedia, Genealogy, and Tradition* (Notre Dame, IN: University of Notre Dame Press, 1990), 125.

necessary and fruitful, for example, if there were ever an age that was intent upon demystification of the body, of sexual difference, of marriage and family etc., -like our age. John Paul reopened the question in just this circumstance, to deal with a major theological problem of our day. He faced different and difficult theological challenges and he met them using a different methodology, a different anthropology and a different epistemology from those used by Aquinas or Augustine, and he reached different conclusions.

Bertrand de Margerie argues that the major reason the family unit is not more widely accepted as analogous to the Blessed Trinity is Augustine's rejection of the analogy in *De Trinitatae* and Aquinas' rejection in his *Summa Theologica*. Likening the family to the Blessed Trinity has been sidelined in theology largely due to the enormous influence of Augustine and Aquinas. At the end of the twentieth century, however, Saint John Paul's likening of the family to the Blessed Trinity has catapulted this anthropological proposition to the front and center position in Catholic theology. A knowledgeable theologian recently said: "It (The *Theology of the Body*) is the only game in town."[69] How this revival broke upon the stage in the twentieth Century is the story of the *Theology of the Body's* development of the doctrine of *Humanae Vitae*.

I.1 Summary

Part I.1 consisted of an illustrative sample of traditional anthropological proposals by theologians and philosophers over great spans of time from the first centuries of the Church up to the scholastic period. It contains different understandings concerning: God's activity in creating man; the *imago Dei*, the meaning of the image and likeness of God in man; man's spiritual aspect, mind, spirit or soul; his body and sex; the purpose of marriage; and more, all excerpted from larger narratives of origin and in

---

[69] Portier, William L., The Ann Spearin Chair of Catholic Theology at the University of Dayton

the overarching context of the mysteries of Creation, Redemption and Sanctification.

We encountered dual creations in Philo, Origin and Gregory of Nyssa; distinctions between image and likeness of God in Origin and Irenaeus; notions of resurrected bodies that are spiritualized and sexually undifferentiated in Origin, Gregory of Nyssa, and Maximus. There were explanations of the body as rooted in evil from Philo and Origin; and, an explanation of the body as participating in the *imago Dei* in Irenaeus and John Chrysostom; and an explanation of the body as the means of deification in Maximus.

We encountered the logos of Neo-Platonism in Philo and the Logos as the true *imago Dei*, Christ, in Gregory of Nyssa. We encountered symbolic relationships between the family and the Blessed Trinity understood in different ways by Gregory Nazianzus, John Chrysostom, Augustine, and Aquinas. We encountered marriage as uncorrupted by the fall and the body as participating in *theosis* or divinization in Athanasius, and encountered the one flesh union of man and woman as the *imago Dei* in Chrysostom. These brief sketches illustrate the persistence and vitality of questions of theological anthropology, the variety of responses, and theology's long and vigorous effort to answer the psalmist's question: "what is man that you are mindful of him?"

I.2 Natural Law

Natural law is central to the theological debates for and against the moral doctrine of *Humanae Vitae*. Catholic tradition upholds natural law as a philosophical idea, supported by revelation. Natural law holds that creatures realize fulfillment by acting according to laws written in their natures and that these laws are accessible to human reason. Every creature fulfills its reason for being by acting according to its nature. This idea grounds natural law theory. When applied to human acts it is an ethical standard. The gospel is the ethical standard par excellence to the faithful; however, natural law is a reliable ethical standard accessible to all. Revelation and natural law are mutually supportive in the Catholic understanding and cannot contradict one another.

In recent years, leading Catholic theologians invited leaders of the great religious and wisdom traditions to join in a dialog about ethics. In 2009 the International Theological Commission (ITC), under the Roman Congregation for the Doctrine of the Faith (CDF), published a document entitled: *In Search of a Universal Ethic: A New Look at the Natural Law.*[70] The document, intended as an initial contribution to the dialog, is a contemporary Catholic presentation of the natural law. This chapter considers the foundations of the natural law according to the ITC document.

I.2a ITC Document Overview

In Search of a Universal Ethic: A New Look at the Natural Law.

The ITC document contains an introduction, five chapters and a conclusion. The introduction: "invite[s] all those pondering the ultimate foundations of ethics…to consider the resources that a renewed presentation of the doctrine of the natural law contains."[71] It aims to present a new look at a natural law ethic as a contribution to the search for a universal ethic. "It invites the great religions, sapiential and philosophical traditions of humanity to undertake an analogous work…in order to reach a common recognition of universal norms based on a rational approach to reality"[72]

Chapter I proposes that a version of the golden rule, to do unto others what you would have them do unto you, can be found in the great religions (Judaism, Christianity, Islam) and wisdom traditions of the world (Hinduism, Buddhism, Taoism, Greco-Roman philosophy, and African

---

[70] Various, *In Search of a Universal Ethic: A New Look at the Natural Law.*

[71] Ibid., 9.

[72] Ibid., 116.

traditions). According to the document, this is evidence of a common human moral patrimony and "One is justified to see in this consensus a manifestation of that which – beyond the diversity of cultures – is the human in the human being, namely "human nature."[73] The chapter also discusses intellectual movements opposed to this moral patrimony and to a universal ethic. These are identified as: voluntarism; radical secularization that dismisses both revelation and the great wisdom traditions; and radical rationalism that reduces our common moral patrimony to a deductive moral code. These intellectual movements marginalize revelation and the great wisdom traditions.

Chapter II explains how individual human persons come to grasp fundamental moral values through experience. From birth to maturity humans experience and are taught in familial and social settings to distinguish activities that lead to happiness and fulfillment from those that do not. This experiential learning comports with St. Thomas Aquinas' first principle of practical reason, -that good is to be done and pursued and evil is to be avoided. Thus, a gradually acquired ability to weigh good and evil is the basis for dialogue with persons of other cultural or religious commitments.

Chapter III focuses on the philosophical foundations underpinning the natural law. The foundations are anthropological and ontological. Anthropology is presented in terms of "constants that characterize a successful humanization of the person and a harmonious social life."[74] Ontology is presented thus: "…only the recognition of the metaphysical dimension of the real can give to natural law its full and complete philosophical justification."[75] The chapter proposes an ontological distinction between contingent and necessary being, to which all contingent being tends for fulfillment. In the Christian understanding, personal freedom tends to fulfillment "in a free and gratuitous relationship

---

[73] Ibid., 36.
[74] Ibid., 61.
[75] Ibid., 62.

of love with God."[76] Some contemporary philosophical challenges to this grounding of natural law in a harmonious relationship between God, man and nature, are also explained.

Chapter IV considers the social and political dimensions of the natural law which recognizes the human person as a social being who promotes the common good in the civil and political orders. In social and political domains, the natural law clarifies the distinction between political and religious spheres and clarifies just relationships between societies and governments.

Chapter V considers the autonomy of the natural law from creedal commitments despite its integral harmony with Christianity's theological commitments. It characterizes natural law as ultimately fulfilled through the grace of Jesus Christ, notwithstanding its intelligibility and accessibility to believers and nonbelievers alike.

The conclusion reiterates the invitation to all to join in the search for a universal ethic. It refers to the United Nations Charter and celebrates the fact that:

> After the Second World War, the nations of the entire world were able to create a *Universal Declaration of Human Rights*, which implicitly suggests that the source of unalienable human rights is found in the dignity of every human person.[77]

And, concludes that: "The present contribution has no other aim than that of helping to reflect on this source of personal and collective morality.[78]

---

[76] Ibid., 66.

[77] Ibid., 115.

[78] Ibid.

I.2b Anthropology and Ontology of the ITC Document

The ITC document explains the anthropological justification of natural law as follows: "The idea of a natural law is justified, first of all, on the level of the reflective observation of the anthropological constants that characterize a successful humanization of the person and a harmonious social life."[79]

The document doesn't identify or develop what is meant by anthropological constants, successfully humanized persons, or harmonious social lives. It follows this vague justification for the idea of natural law with descriptions of capabilities or powers by which the human person can progress to human fulfillment. For example:

> The human person is capable of knowledge and of love; he is endowed with freedom, capable of entering into communion with others and called by God to a destiny that transcends the finalities of physical nature. He fulfills himself in a free and gratuitous relationship of love with God that is realized in a history. [80]

The document explains the anthropological foundation of natural law in two ways:

On the one hand, according to the definition of Boethius, taken up again by scholastic theology, the person is an "individual substance of a rational nature." It refers to the uniqueness of an ontological subject who, being of a spiritual nature enjoys a dignity and an autonomy that is manifested in self-consciousness and in free dominion over his actions. Furthermore, the person is manifested in his capacity to enter into relation. He displays his action in the order of intersubjectivity and communion in love.[81]

---

[79] Ibid., 61.
[80] Ibid., 66.
[81] Ibid., 67.

This description first references the Boethian 'individual substance of a rational nature' anthropology and then interprets the rational nature broadly to include capabilities to enter into relation, and communion in love, in an order of inter-subjectivity. It is unclear whether the capability to enter into relation and communion is integral to a rational nature or instrumental to the rational nature. Instrumentality is suggested by the fact that these capabilities belong to an order of intersubjectivity which is a category that is not further defined or elaborated. So, the rational and relational capacities or powers do not appear to be integrated in a single clear and unambiguous anthropological definition firmly grounding natural law theory.

On the other hand, the document does articulate, with clarity and confidence, an integrated and unified ontological justification of natural law theory. It states: "Nevertheless, only the recognition of the metaphysical dimension of the real can give to natural law its full and complete philosophical justification."[82] The document continues:

> To give the notion of the natural law all its meaning and strength as the foundation of a universal ethic, a perspective of wisdom needs to be promoted, belonging properly to the metaphysical order, and capable of simultaneously including God, the cosmos and the human person, in order to reconcile them in the analogical unity of being, thanks to the idea of creation as participation.[83]

The document's grounding of natural law theory anthropologically and ontologically raises questions. Does the document actually propose a coherent anthropological foundation and justification for natural law theory? Or, does it propose that a metaphysics of the analogical unity of

---

[82] Ibid., 62.
[83] Ibid., 76.

being is an adequate foundation to justify natural law theory independent of a more coherent anthropology?

As we shall see, John Paul considered anthropological foundations to be of the first importance in his philosophical and theological work, particularly in the *Theology of the Body*, in which he brings aspects of the idea of *Humanae Vitae* into consistency and form by proposing a more complete and coherent anthropology upon which to ground its moral doctrine.

I.2c Commentary on the ITC Document

Theologians commenting on the ITC document have drawn attention to its anthropological ambiguity. Three in particular addressed the issue in different ways: the first, Serge-Thomas Bonino O.P., one of the document's principal authors; the second, Gilbert Meilaender, a prominent reform theologian; and the third, Livio Melina, the former dean of the Roman session of the John Paul II Institute for the study of marriage and family.

Serge-Thomas Bonino O.P., a principal author of the document, speaking of the deliberations that led to the ITC document, commented that its authors deepened the notion of natural law in two complimentary directions. The first direction Bonino describes as follows:

> Some wanted to overcome the impasse of a rationalistic, modern approach to natural law, founded on an ahistorical and *a priori* conception of human nature that had widely contaminated Catholic moral theology. They thus returned to the origins of the doctrine, especially as found in St. Thomas Aquinas. They worked to better place the doctrine of natural law within the whole framework of Thomistic thought. The Thomistic doctrine of natural law, as a participation in the eternal law (i.e. in God's plans for the world), is inseparable from

a metaphysics of creation. Moreover, it is part of a view of morality identified by attraction to happiness, the role of the virtues, the primacy of grace, and the like.[84]

Bonino describes the second direction as follows:

> Others, following the example of Pope John Paul II, elaborated a personalist presentation of the doctrine of natural law. Rejecting the idea of the human subject's total passive submission to an impersonal nature, they articulated in a more satisfactory manner the relationship between the person as the subject of moral autonomy and nature as an expression of divine thinking.[85]

It is true that a 'Thomistic doctrine of natural law...is inseparable from a metaphysics of creation,' and 'a more satisfactory articulation of the relationship between the person as the subject of moral autonomy and nature as an expression of divine thinking,' are complimentary directions. However, it is not clear that their complementarity is adequately developed in the document. They appear, as in Bonino's commentary, to be competing anthropological approaches. Ambivalent, ambiguous or competing anthropologies call into question the integrity of the natural law presentation. To recognize anthropology and metaphysics as the philosophical foundation and justification of natural law is to call for an integral anthropology and metaphysics. It is not clear that this document presents an integral anthropology and metaphysics.

---

[84] O.P. Serge-Thomas Bonino, "An Introduction to the Document *in Search of a Universal Ethic: A New Look at the Natural Law*," in *Searching for a Universal Ethic: Multidisciplinary, Ecumenical, and Interfaith Responses to the Catholic Natural Law Tradition*, ed. John Berkman and William C. Mattison III (Grand Rapida: William B. Eerdmans, 2014), 96.

[85] Ibid.

Gilbert Meilaender places anthropology first among his misgivings about the document. Meilaender explains:

> Perhaps this essentially Thomistic theory, 'belonging properly to the metaphysical order' does, in fact, unpack the underlying structure of the objective moral law. Yet it seems, at least to me, to lack the metaphysical ground of which it speaks. While rejecting voluntarism and anthropological dualism, the document does relatively little to describe what it calls 'the human in the human being.' It might have been wise to begin lower to the ground, with basic reflection on the nature of human life. [86]

Meilaender further stresses his point: "There is, I repeat, nothing wrong with attempting to develop a theory that adequately outlines a universal theory of objective moral law, although doing so requires a richer anthropology than this document provides.[87]

By calling for a 'richer anthropology than this document provides' I understand Meilaender to be saying that by not describing what is meant by the 'human in the human being,' the document glosses over the required anthropological foundation to utilize a metaphysical foundation without elaborating its anthropological grounding. That is what I understand him to mean by saying 'It might have been wise to begin lower to the ground, with basic reflection on the nature of human life.'

Livio Melina proposes a radically renewed personalistic interpretation of the natural law. He calls for an alternative explication centered on personal action. He understands natural law as a grammar of action that

---

[86] Gilbert Meilaender, "Can't We All Just Get Along?," in *Searching for a Universal Ethic: Multidisciplinary, Ecumenical, and Interfaith Responses to the Catholic Natural Law Tradition*, ed. John Berkman and William C. Mattison III (Grand Rapids: William B. Eerdmans, 2014), 223.

[87] Ibid., 224.

guarantees the truth of the communication among persons.[88] He describes the trajectory of his reasoning:

> We will look at the experience of the body, in which action is rooted, and the experience of interpersonal relations in the network in which action is inserted, proposing a "pragmatics" of love, which avoids the extrinsicism of both naturalism and rationalism. In this way we will arrive at a renewed interpretation of the natural law, according to which the fundamental human goods, which give orientation to the spontaneous inclinations of human nature, acquire an original moral meaning – the dynamic and personalistic horizon of love.[89]

To summarize Melina: natural law is about action; human action is rooted in the body; action occurs in the network of interpersonal relations; the spontaneous inclinations of human nature are oriented to fundamental human goods; and, these spontaneous inclinations acquire moral meaning in the dynamic and personalistic horizon of love

This understanding disfavors naturalistic and rationalistic analyses because they are extrinsic to action. Whereas action itself communicates comprehensively, a naturalistic or rationalistic grammar or language about human action is always reductive of what action itself communicates. Therefore, Melina believes a pragmatics of love as the moral criterion (rather than nature or reason), opens natural law theory to a comprehensive account of action in its superabundant imminent, transcendent, and transformative effects that go beyond the range and reach of naturalistic and rationalistic analyses.

---

[88] Livio Melina, "Pragmatic and Christological Foundations of Natural Law," in *Searching for a Universal Ethic: Multidisciplinary, Ecumenical, and Interfaith Responses to the Catholic Natural Law Tradition*, ed. John Berkman and William C. Mattison III (Grand Rapids: William B Eerdmans, 2014), 293.
[89] Ibid., 293-4.

Melina offers an alternative to the ITC document's characterization of natural law theory proposing instead a theory worked out in the contexts of the body, Christology, creation, redemption and sanctification. He affirms natural law theory, but disfavors nature and reason as primary criteria, favoring instead, a personalistic criterion of love.[90]

I.2d Relevance of the ITC Document

In summary, The International Theological Commission under the auspices of the Congregation for the Doctrine of the Faith published a document in 2009 entitled *In Search of a Universal Ethic: A New Look at the Natural Law*. The document locates the philosophical foundation and justification for natural law theory in anthropology and metaphysics. It identifies the metaphysical foundation and justification in a realist metaphysics of being. Its identification of an anthropological foundation and justification of natural law theory is ambivalent. *Humanae Vitae* cited the authority of the natural law in its moral argument prohibiting the contraception of conjugal acts. An imbroglio following *Humanae Vitae's* promulgation centered on just such questions concerning how to understand and interpret the anthropological foundations of the natural law.

I.3 Personalism

This chapter discusses personalism and the personalist perspective from which the *Theology of the Body* develops the anthropological foundation of *Humanae Vitae*.

Humanae Vitae supports its moral doctrine theologically and philosophically. Theologically it argues from revelation, from the teaching

---

[90] Karol Wojtyla, *Love and Responsibility*, trans. H. T. Willetts (San Francisco: Ignatius Press, 1960), 41.

authority of the magisterium and from the reliable guidance of tradition. Philosophically it argues from the authority of natural law and draws inferences from rational analyses. As illustrated in the preceding chapter, however, natural law can be construed as secure in its metaphysical foundation and justification, but ambivalent in its anthropological foundation and justification. Anthropological ambiguity leaves a wide opening for debate. The *Theology of the Body* aims to close this opening.

The *Theology of the Body* deepens the anthropological foundation and justification supporting *Humanae Vitae's* moral doctrine by securing its personalistic grounding to supplement and complement its naturalistic and rationalistic groundings.

The *Theology of the Body* takes issue with the Boethian anthropology which defines the human person as an 'individual substance of a rational nature.' It agrees that man is an individual substance of a rational nature. However, this definition excludes sexual difference which is ineliminable according to the *Theology of the Body*. Consequently, the *Theology of the Body* proposes an understanding of the human person that accounts for sexual difference to complete *Humanae Vitae's* natural and rational anthropological foundation and justification.

The theological controversy surrounding *Humanae Vitae* centered on arguments about how nature and reason support or do not support the encyclical's doctrinal moral imperative. These are philosophical questions. They raise the specter of whether the natural law as understood and applied in *Humanae Vitae* is anthropologically adequate, and whether reason applied abstractly and casuistically is rationally adequate. Opponents criticized the encyclical's application of natural law and moral reasoning for being out of touch with ordinary experience. Arguments were made on both sides of the question from a perspective of nature and abstract rationality constrained by a largely unchallenged ambivalent anthropology. The way forward called for a deepening of the Boethian anthropology and moral analyses commensurate with that deeper anthropology.

John Paul recognized the importance of the questions raised by *Humanae Vitae*, their urgency, and the difficulty of resolving them. His response, the *Theology of the Body*, takes up this challenge in a personalist perspective.

I.3a Origins of Personalism

Christianity is ever committed to truth. Philosophy is also committed to truth. Christian theology accepts the truth of philosophy subject to faith in a higher revealed truth. John Paul II reminded us that theology is mediated by philosophy which is the conceptual language *par excellence.*[91] For example, the Church Fathers generally mediated theology through Platonic idealism and medieval scholastic theologians mediated theology largely through Aristotelian realism. John Paul also reminded us that theology can come to the aid of philosophy when philosophy encounters limits.[92] One such contribution to philosophy is the concept of what it means to be a person. The story of how this came about is the story of the origin of our current understanding of personhood.

The drama of Christian theology opening a philosophical horizon played out in the early Christian centuries as theologians pondered not only the mysteries of creation *ex nihilo*, but also the mystery of one God that is Father, Son and Holy Spirit, and the mystery of Christ as true God and true man.

The starting point for the Greek philosophy was the world around us which they understood to be an eternal cosmos. Christian thinkers, however, understood the cosmos to be created *ex nihilo*, -from nothing. A cosmos created from nothing, of course, could not be eternal. It implied a beginning. A beginning implied a creator, which implied an uncreated

---

[91] Pope John Paul II, *Man and Woman He Created Them; a Theology of the Body*, trans. Michael Waldstein (Boston: Pauline Books & Media, 2006), 140 ff.

[92] Pope John Paul II, *Fides Et Ratio: Encyclical on Faith and Reason* (1999), http://w2.vatican.va/content/john-paul-ii/en/encyclicals/documents/hf_jp-ii_enc_14091998_fides-et-ratio.html.

subject, somehow outside the cosmos, with intelligence and freedom, in short, an eternal supreme being.

In addition to accepting the implications of creation *ex nihilo*, ecumenical councils labored to explain the triune God, Father, Son and Holy Spirit, and Christ as true God and true man. The ecumenical councils ultimately explained the Blessed Trinity as one in substance, and three in *persons*, and they ultimately explained Christ as having two natures, one divine and one human, in one divine *person*.

These dogmatic definitions, and the idea of creation *ex nihilo*, led philosophy beyond its inherent limitations by offering to the philosophical lexicon a completely new concept, the concept of person, which was far beyond any pre-Christian understanding or use of the term. Likewise, the idea of creation *ex nihilo* opened horizons otherwise beyond the reach of philosophy's self-contained eternally cyclical cosmos. Our modern philosophical understanding of human persons as incommunicable subjects, possessed of unsurpassable dignity, unalienable rights and freedom, is owing to Christian theological reflection on the mysteries of creation *ex nihilo*, the Blessed Trinity and Christ. This is an illustration of how theology helped philosophy surpass its methodological limitations and opened a horizon in the form of a new and profound understanding of personal existence.

The *Theology of the Body* proposes a theological anthropology in a personalist perspective. The personalist perspective seeks to increase our understanding of the meaning of personhood. Personalism includes personalistic principles such as: human persons are more than members of a species; each individual person is unique and unrepeatable; persons are incommunicable, which means that my personhood is unique to me, belongs to me, is me, and cannot be taken from me by another; interiority, which is our experience of our own selves as persons; inter-subjectivity, which identifies persons according to their relationships, and through which persons form communities in inter-personal communion.

Personalist philosophers and theologians approach questions of ethics, including norms and moral analysis, epistemology, anthropology and ontology or metaphysics, in a personalist perspective. The fact that the very meaning of person itself comes to us from Christian theology's struggle to understand the Christian mysteries of creation *ex nihilo*, the Blessed Trinity and Christ true God and true man, is the central justification of the whole argument of the *Theology of the Body*. This fact illuminates an irreducible affinity between God and man, in as much as we have our concept of human personhood only because of Christian reflection on God. Our self-understanding is immeasurably ennobled due to that historical reflection. The *Theology of the Body* develops this affinity as its central thesis. Before engaging the personalism of the *Theology of the Body*, the history of the development of personalism warrants further consideration.

In Greco-Roman society, the words for person, *prosopon* and *persona* respectively, denoted: for the Greeks, the role or function of an individual within the eternal, deterministic, cyclical, cosmic order of the universe; and denoted for the Romans, the role an individual played not so much in the cosmic order of the universe as in the structure and organization of Roman society, the all-important Roman state.

John Zizioulas, Metropolitan of Pergamon in the Ecumenical Patriarchate of Constantinople, explains that the Judeo-Christian notion of creation *ex nihilo* increasingly took hold in the Greco-Roman world. This was disruptive to the prevailing notion of person because in the Christian understanding, reality was not determined by the cosmos or the state. A cosmos created *ex nihilo* was a contingent universe and implied a creator's free action. The idea of free action eroded the prevailing determinism. At the same time the Greek Fathers of the Church struggled to make Christianity's confession of one God who was Father, Son and Holy Spirit intelligible. Greek philosophy lacked a helpful vocabulary. If the Greek term *prosopon* were used for Father, Son and Holy Spirit, it would only distinguish different roles played by the one God, and would further the heresy of Sabellianism.[93]

---

[93] John D. Zizioulas, *Being as Communion* (Crestwood, NY: St. Vladimir's Press, 1985), 35 ff.

The problem is that the New Testament reveals Christ the Son of God made man, and also reveals God as Father, as Son and as Holy Spirit, though there is only one God. In time, the dogmatic definition of the Blessed Trinity as three persons in one God gave an entirely new meaning to the term person. According to the catechism of the Catholic Church:

> In order to articulate the dogma of the Trinity, the Church had to develop her own terminology with the help of certain notions of philosophical origin: "substance", "person" or "hypostasis", "relation" and so on. In doing this, she did not submit the faith to human wisdom, but gave a new and unprecedented meaning to these terms, which from then on would be used to signify an ineffable mystery, "infinitely beyond all that we can humanly understand."[94]

Joseph Ratzinger, Pope Benedict XVI, explains how, in a variety of ways, our contemporary understanding of the term 'person,' has its origin in Christian faith. The Church gave the term 'person' a whole new meaning by adopting the term to represent the Father, Son and Holy Spirit, in the dogmatic definition of the Blessed Trinity. Our contemporary understanding and use of the term 'person,' originated in this dogmatic definition. Ratzinger explains this as one example of how Christian faith and theology contribute powerfully to philosophy:

> The concept of person as well as the idea that stands behind this concept is a product of Christian theology.... The concept of person is one of the contributions to human thought made possible and provided by Christian faith....In my judgment one cannot, therefore, know

---

[94] *Catechism of the Catholic Church* (2016), accessed May 2016, http://www.vatican.va/archive/ENG0015/_INDEX.HTM.

what "person" most truly means without fathoming this origin.[95]

Ratzinger identifies Tertullian (Born c.155, Died c. 220) as the original source of the contemporary concept of "person." "Thus it was Tertullian who gave the West its formula for expressing the Christian idea of God. God is *'una substantia-tres personae,'* 'one being in three persons. It was here that the word *person* entered intellectual history for the first time with its full weight."[96]

Ratzinger further points out that the contemporary concept of "person" also grew out of the Old Testament scriptures because it was needed for their interpretation. The literary or poetic device of moving dramatic action forward by creating dialogical speaking roles for mythical figures was a staple of classical theatrics. The search for meaning in the dramatic speeches of these mythical figures was a staple of literary interpretation.

Unsurprisingly, methods of interpreting dramatic roles in plays and poems were applied by exegetes to interpreting dialogs in the scriptures. The Old Testament reveals a God who dialogs with his chosen people. However, and this is the critical point, Christian faith understood that the dialogical role (Greek, *prosopon*; Latin, *persona*) was no mythical character, but the living God in dialog with his people. This too is one of the ways Christianity transformed the common meaning of the word "person" from a role or a function into its contemporary meaning.

As time went on and the Church addressed Trinitarian and Christological controversies in the patristic period, the concept of "person" continued to develop and lend precision to dogmatic formulae. According to Ratzinger:

> ...in order to answer these fundamental questions that arose as soon as faith began to reflect, Christian thought

---

[95] Ratzinger, 439.
[96] Ibid., 440.

made use of the philosophically insignificant or entirely unused concept *"prosopon"* = *"persona."* It thereby gave this word a new meaning and opened up a new dimension of human thought. [97] … In light of this knowledge of God, the true nature of humanity became clear in a new way. (Ratzinger 1990)[98]

In addition to Tertullian's formulation of Trinitarian theology and the transformation of poetic exegesis into a personal biblical exegesis, the concept of person grew out of further developments in Christology. A theological formulation of the mystery of Christ as one divine person who is true God and true man emerged in the Council of Chalcedon in 451:

> This one and the same Jesus Christ, the only-begotten Son [of God] must be confessed to be in two natures, unconfusedly, immutably, indivisibly, inseparably [united], and that without the distinction of natures being taken away by such union, but rather the peculiar property of each nature being preserved and being united in one *Person* …[99]

Joseph Ratzinger insists that our understanding of the concept of person must flow from its fontal theological roots if we are to appreciate the extent to which a personalist understanding of man is fruitful for theology and philosophy: This is why he believes one cannot know what 'person' most truly means without fathoming its origin.[100]

In summary, personalism in philosophy and in theology seeks to understand the meaning of personhood and philosophizes or theologizes

---

[97] Ibid., 439.

[98] Ibid., 443.

[99] "Session 5," *Ecumenical Council IV* (451), http://www.newadvent.org/fathers/3811.htm.

[100] Ratzinger, 440.

in a personalist perspective. Theologians, biblical exegetes and Ecumenical Councils in the early Church transformed the common Greek and Roman meaning of person, *prosopon*, *persona*, from a role in the universe, in a play, or in society, to what we understand by person today. Reading the Bible through the eyes of faith meant that the speaking roles, narrations, orations and prophesies, could not be thought of as mere literary or theatrical techniques, but rather as communication from the living, personal God. Trinitarian theology and Christology commandeered the term 'person' to explain the Father, Son and Holy Spirit in the Blessed Trinity, and the principle of unity in the human and divine natures -without confusion, change, division or separation- in Jesus Christ.

I.3b Personalism and Natural Law

This section discusses characteristics that distinguish personalist anthropology from the Boethian anthropology as adopted by scholastics and featured in the ITC document; *In Search of a Universal Ethic: A New Look at the Natural Law*. Personalist anthropology accepts the Boethian classifications of 'individual substance of a rational nature.' However, personalism holds that the experience of personhood, of being a person, is unique, unrepeatable and incommunicable in each individual. Commenting on the crowding out of this existential personalist view by the Boethian essentialist and substantialist view, Joseph Ratzinger offered an apt metaphor. He said that: "…we have built our closets too small, as it were, and that we must break them open and go on in order to see the whole."[101] The small closet metaphor is also apt for the anthropology underpinning *Humanae Vitae*, which the *Theology of the Body's* personalistic analyses seeks to 'break open and go on in order to see the whole.'

The benefits of enlarging the Boethian essential substantialist view with the existential personalist view come from its interior focus on

---

[101] Ibid. 450

the concrete person in his or her subjective and affective dimensions. These considerations lie outside the scope and range or beyond the reach of substantialist reasoning. For that reason, personalism can supply a broader and deeper anthropological foundation than is featured in the ITC document. The scholastic natural law tradition stressed the objective dimensions of creation and a metaphysics of cosmological being as opposed to personalism which stresses the subjective dimensions of personal being. Personalism turns to the subject to seek to better understand personal existence. According to John Crosby, "This awakening of human beings to personal existence is an epochal event, a sea-change in the way we understand ourselves."[102]

According to Thomas Aquinas, *esse*, to be, is an act of being. Thomas understood existence as an action, and all existing things by virtue of their existing, to be in act. He recognized personal beings as the most perfect in the hierarchy of created beings. Moreover, Thomas considered the act of being to be an act of communication, an act of self-disclosure, and an action reaching toward perfection, or an act of self-fulfillment. All these characteristics of being in Thomistic metaphysics are congenial to personalism. Nevertheless, Aquinas did not develop his philosophical anthropology based on the unique incommunicable self-experience of the human subject considered as a person, -a personalism, as have modern personalists.

Theologically, Thomas understood the personal existence of human beings in natural and supernatural categories. The human person participated in the created natural order of the cosmos. Unlike the rest of the cosmos, however, the human person also participated in the supernatural order by divine grace. This characterization of reality served well prior to the modern age which is characterized by skepticism. We are skeptical of philosophical reasoning, skeptical of creation *ex nihilo* and skeptical of purposefulness in nature. These skepticisms tend to

---

[102] John F. Crosby, "What We Mean by Personalism," (accessed 2016, http://www.thepersonalistproject.org/about_us.

dismiss ethical values derived from nature and hence the moral efficacy of the natural law theory. Insulated from nature, individuals choose or construe hierarchies of ethics autonomously according to criteria that fit their behavior preferences. Ethics disconnected from nature in this way deconstructs cultures, societies and traditions that reflectively and reflexively have deferred to nature in regulating behavior and in ethical reasoning.

As societies, and Western societies in particular, reject nature in ethical reasoning, the more tradition minded seek resources to combat the harms of social deconstruction. The challenge to find effective resources is ultimately a search for a deeper penetration into the mystery of the human person. The quest for a universal ethic is a quest for a deeper understanding of the human person for both natural law theorists and personalists.

I.3c Personalist Perspectives

Insights of contemporary personalist philosophers and theologians illustrate the personalist approach to anthropology, ethics and epistemology. Excerpts from four theologians, Karol Wojtyla, John Zizioulas, Joseph Ratzinger and John Henry Newman are included as samples of personalist approaches to philosophy and theology.

The first excerpts from Karol Wojtyla illustrate how, unlike classical philosophy that begins its reflection with the intelligibility of the cosmos, personalism begins its reflection with the intelligibility and self-understanding of the human person individually and inter-subjectively in communion. The second excerpt from John Zizioulas illustrates a personalist approach to ontology. The third excerpt from Newman illustrates a personalist approach to ethics. Excerpts from the fourth theologian, Ratzinger, illustrate some historical advances and setbacks to the personalist approach in Christian theology.

WOJTYLA

Personalism does not replace or displace classical metaphysics of being or Boethian anthropology but seeks to complete them both, or to enlarge the closet, to borrow Ratzinger's metaphor. The main idea is stated clearly by Karol Wojtyla, speaking as a philosopher:

> The experience of the human being cannot be derived by way of cosmological reduction; we must pause at the irreducible, at that which is unique and unrepeatable in each human being, by virtue of which he or she is not just *a particular human being* – an individual of a certain species – but a *personal subject*. Only then do we get a true and complete picture of the human being. We cannot complete this picture through reduction alone; we also cannot remain within the framework of the irreducible alone (for then we would be unable to get beyond the pure self). The one must be cognitively supplemented with the other. Nevertheless, given the variety of circumstances of the real existence of human beings, we must always leave the greater space in this cognitive effort for the irreducible; we must, as it were, give the irreducible the upper hand when thinking about the human being, both in theory and in practice. For the irreducible also refers to everything in the human being that is invisible and wholly internal and whereby each human being, myself included, is an "eyewitness" of his or her own self – of his or her own humanity and person.[103]

---

[103] Karol Wojtyla, *Person and Community*, trans. Theresa Sandok OSM, vol. 4, *Catholic Thought from Lublin* (NY: Peter Lang, 1993), 214.

To 'give the irreducible the upper hand when thinking about the human being, both in theory and in practice,' and to 'leave the greater space…for the irreducible' is to acknowledge incompleteness in substantialist anthropology and cosmological reductive ethical analyses, and to claim a higher ground, a more decisive role and a greater space, for personalistic analyses.

Applied to natural law theory, this claim would favor and afford the greater space to the irreducible, existentialist, personalist anthropology than to substantialist ethical reasoning. The personalist approach enlarges, broadens and deepens the foundation and justification for ethical reasoning. Wojtyla, in fact, proposed a universal personalistic ethic in his philosophical work, *Love and Responsibility* in which he formulated: "the person is the good toward which the only proper and adequate attitude is love."

Another relevant dimension of Wojtyla's thought is his understanding of communion, particularly the *communio personarum* or communion of persons. Wojtyla wrote:

> By 'community' I understand "that which unites." In the *I–thou* relationship, an authentic interpersonal community develops (regardless of its form or variety) if the *I* and the *thou* abide in a mutual affirmation of the transcendent value of the person (a value that may be called *dignity*) and confirm this by their acts. Only such a relationship seems to deserve the name *communio personarum*.[104]

As we shall see, Wojtyla's understanding of community and communion is central to the *Theology of the Body's* development of *Humanae Vitae*.

---

[104] Ibid., 246.

ZIZIOULAS

John Zizioulas further illuminates notions of person, communion and being. According to Zizioulas, persons are 'the ontological principle' or cause of beings. As we saw above in discussing creation *ex nihilo*, by virtue of the act of creation the existence of the world is not eternal and not necessary; rather, it is a result of freedom, the product of a free act. "Not only was the being of the world traced back to personal freedom, but *the being of God Himself* was identified with the person."[105]

NEWMAN

Another expression of personalism can be seen, in Blessed John Henry Newman's ethical analysis of conscience and moral obligation. We said that Karol Wojtyla proposed a universal personalist ethic or norm, that 'the person is the good toward which the only proper and adequate attitude is love.' Newman had drawn attention to precisely this personalist dynamic in the self-assessment of sinfulness in human wrongdoing. John Crosby describes Newman's insight as follows:

> Conscience is not just a matter of morality for Newman; moral obligation is also something distinctly religious; a *mysterium tremendum* breaks through in moral obligation filling Newman with numinous (*i.e.* spiritual, religious, divine, holy, sacred) dread. When we do wrong, our conscience registers not just *wrongdoing* but *sinfulness*, which is a numinous category; the wrong we do, once exposed to the light of the numinous and the holy, takes

---

[105] Zizioulas, 40.

on the uncleanness of sin…We experience our wrongdoing
as sin whenever we confront it with the holy.[106]

This unfolding of conscience, the deepest interiority of personal
subjects was for Newman, not merely a moral but a religious experience. It
exceeds morality and is entirely different and separate from the dry, sober,
abstract, rational, deontological ethical analyses we find in the application
of natural law theory. Instead, it is the shuddering of conscience at the
reality of offending God in an inter-personal way.

RATZINGER

Joseph Ratzinger draws attention to Richard of St. Victor's contribution
to personalism at the beginning of the Middle Ages. "Richard…found
a concept of person derived from within Christianity when he defined a
person as…the incommunicably proper existence of spiritual nature. This
definition correctly sees that in its theological meaning "person does not
lie on the level of essence, but of existence."[107] Richard's definition applies
to the Persons of the Blessed Trinity, to angels and to man. Richard added
a personalist anthropological understanding on the level of existence to
Boethius' substantialist anthropological understanding on the level of
essence or substance. By identifying Persons in the Blessed Trinity with
existence rather than essence, Richard discovered the ground of free divine
action. Divine action is the activity of Personal freedom in interpersonal
communion. This theological ground of free Personal action in inter-
personal communion accounts for all of creation. By understanding that
persons are incommunicable, that their personhood cannot be taken from
them, we can also understand that acts of personal inter-communion
are necessarily free acts, and therefore can only occur in the dimension

---

[106] John F. Crosby, *The Personalism of John Henry Newman* (Washington DC:
Catholic University of America Press, 2014), 197-8.
[107] Ratzinger, 449.

of gift. In this schema, theologically and anthropologically, free acts of communion constitute persons. Ratzinger explains:

> In other words, the spirit comes to itself in the other, it becomes completely itself the more it is with the other, with God. And again, formulated the other way around, because this idea seems important to me: relativity toward the other constitutes the human person. The human person is the event or being of relativity. The more the person's relativity aims totally and directly at its final goal, at transcendence, the more the person is itself.[108]

Ratzinger explains that the consequences of Richard of Saint Victor's contribution of an existential understanding of 'person' were not fully developed in scholastic theology or philosophy:

> In antiquity, philosophy was limited entirely to the level of essence. Scholastic theology developed categories of existence out of this contribution given by Christian faith to the human mind. Its defect was that it limited these categories to Christology and the doctrine of the Trinity and did not make them fruitful in the whole extent of spiritual reality. This seems to me also the limit of St. Thomas in the matter, namely, that within theology he operates, with Richard of St. Victor, on the level of existence, but treats the whole thing as a theological exception, as it were. In philosophy, however, he remains faithful to the different approach of pre- Christian philosophy.[109]

---

108 Ibid., 452.
109 Ibid., 449.

Regarding personalism in St. Thomas, Ratzinger notes that Thomas' applies Richard of St. Victor's spiritual and existential understanding of personhood to the theology of the Blessed Trinity and Christology, but applies the Boethian substantialist and essentialist understanding to his philosophy of human persons. Ratzinger understates the magnitude of this discontinuity by calling it a defect. However, he does not understate its deleterious consequences. He explains the full magnitude of the consequences of this defect as follows:

> The contribution of Christian faith to the whole of human thought is not realized; it remains at first detached from it as a theological exception, although it is precisely the meaning of this new element to call into question the whole of human thought and set it on a new course.[110]

Aquinas' 'defect', according to Ratzinger, was to opt for a Boethian philosophical anthropology. As a consequence of this 'defect' Aquinas veered away from the unique, incommunicable, existential, subjectivity of each individual person. These are the irreducible personal dimensions which, Wojtyla insists, should be given the upper hand.

According to Ratzinger, this defect remains largely unrecognized. It would seem to be a difficulty for any unwary theologian seeking to reconcile Thomism with the personalism animating the *Theology of the Body*. In the *Theology of the Body*, Richard of St. Victor's spiritual existential understanding of the human person applies to the Blessed Trinity, to Christology, and to the human person. Consequently, the *Theology of the Body's* anthropology is rooted in Trinitarian and Christological theology rather than substantialist, essentialist classical philosophy, in which, according to Ratzinger, Thomas' philosophy of the human person is grounded.[111]

---

[110] Ibid.
[111] Ibid.

Ratzinger is also pointedly critical of Saint Augustine's *De Trinitate*. He criticizes Augustine's opting for an intra-psychic Trinitarian image as 'decisive mistake' with grave consequences. Ratzinger makes it abundantly clear that this choice was unfortunate, because from that point forward Catholic theology reflected an intra-psychic individualism to represent the image of God in man rather than opting for the inter-subjective, inter-personal communitarian relations in the Trinity: "...he committed a decisive mistake...In his interpretation he projected the divine persons into the interior life of the human person and affirmed that the intra-psychic processes correspond to these persons. (Ratzinger 1990)[112]

For Ratzinger, this mistake also had far reaching consequences. It exerted a negative influence on theology by emphasizing the oneness of God at the expense of the plurality of God, and the communitarian dimensions of theology lost out to an excess of its individual dimension. According to Ratzinger:

> It was indeed as a result of Augustine's doctrine of the Trinity that the persons of God were closed wholly into God's interior. Toward the outside, God became a simple "I" and the whole dimension of "we" lost its place in theology.[113]

Ratzinger understands Augustine's psychological analogy to the Trinity to be a negative influence on his theological anthropology. Its characteristics ushered a self-enclosed, self-referential, understanding of the human person into Christianity. It is a 'decisive mistake' that steers Augustine's theological anthropology toward individualism and away from a relational understanding of man.

In a personalistic perspective, Aquinas' anthropological account crowds out what is unique and unrepeatable in each human being, that

---

[112] Ibid., 405.
[113] Ibid., 454.

is, subjectivity. Augustine, on the other hand, crowds out the inter-personal dimension, that is, intersubjectivity. The *Theology of the Body* proposes a remedy to what Ratzinger characterizes as Aquinas' 'defect', and Augustine's 'decisive mistake'.

The first three chapters presented three main ideas: the first, a variety of narratives to illustrate how theological anthropology seeks to explain the mystery of man from creation onward; the second, a contemporary proposal of natural law theory as the foundation of ethics; the third, the origins of personalism and examples of how personalist philosophers and theologians approach anthropology and ethics in ways that distinguishes them from natural law theorists.

Before proceeding, to compare the structures and strategies, differences and commonalities in the arguments made by *Humanae Vitae* and the *Theology of the Body* in Parts II and III, there are concerns about the *bona fides* of the *Theology of the Body* as creditable theology and its qualifications as a source of doctrine or doctrinal development. Its argument, its philosophical grounding and its theological method are all questioned. This is discussed in Part I.4 under the heading of first philosophy. Another concern is its level of authority. If John Paul II intended to develop doctrine wouldn't he have chosen a more authoritative way of communicating his proposal than catechetical talks to his Wednesday audiences? The authority of the *Theology of the Body* is discussed in Part I.5

I.4 First Philosophy

Introduction

Anthropology, natural law and personalism represent very broad areas of philosophy and theology and were introduced because they relate to *Humanae Vitae* and the *Theology of the Body*. A lot more might be said in each of these areas but a brief introduction is all that is needed to advance the thesis. The essential ideas are that: first, anthropology is foundational for all areas of theology and is open to development today just as it was in the early Christian centuries; second, there is a strong commitment to Boethian anthropology, natural law theory and an ontology of being as the basic foundations of Catholic moral theology and ethics; and third, many modern philosophers and theologians question whether Boethian anthropology, natural law theory and an ontology of being, by themselves, suffice as an adequate foundation for moral theology and ethics, or, do they require enrichment by personalist perspectives.

First Philosophy; Ontology; Metaphysics

First philosophy, also called ontology or metaphysics, seeks to identify what is primary. An economic model may serve as a useful metaphor. In an economic model, capital is invested in labor and raw materials. Labor is applied to raw materials to create products that can be converted back into capital. In the philosophical enterprise capital is truth. The world and the machinations of the philosopher represent raw material and labor. Philosophers apply their craft to the world to produce the truth of things. Their products are examined for their truth, and what is judged to be true is added back into capital.

So far, neither capital, nor labor nor raw material qualifies as primary because they are dormant unless an entrepreneur acts on an impetus to profit. He acts on this impetus by examining everything he owns and choosing his surest asset for seed capital. The philosopher acts on his impetus for true knowledge. He examines everything he knows and chooses for his seed capital what he is most sure will make the world intelligible.

The act of choosing what is most sure to make the world intelligible is the task of first philosophy. First philosophy asks the question: what is the ultimate criterion of intelligibility? The answer requires a judgment. The judgment is a proposition of first philosophy. Some say the ultimate criterion of intelligibility is being. Some say it is forms or essences. Some say it is unity. Some say it is consciousness. Some say it is utility or function. Some say it is love.

Two Paths, Being and Truth

At this point it may be good to look at the Thomistic synthesis from a foundational viewpoint. According to Alasdair MacIntyre, Thomas worked out the philosophical and theological blueprint for his synthesis in what became *De Veritate* and *De Ente et Essentia*. According to MacIntyre:

> ...*De Veritatae* and *De Ente et Essentia* are philosophical dictionaries in which in the one case the various uses of 'true' and 'truth 'are spelled out and related both to each other and to other key terms, and in the other, similarly, the various uses of 'being' and of 'essence.'

> In both works there is an underlying recognition not only that each of these sets of uses is related analogically, but that there is a primary application of each and that it is to God. It is from God as truth, *veritas*, that all other 'truths' and 'trues' flow; it is from God as being, *esse*, that all that is, insofar as it is, derives.[114]

Given this structure there appear to be two roads for metaphysicians to travel to get to the same place. The one is the road of causality, teleology and predication, and is well traveled. The other road is the road of the true, and the truth, and of truths, the road less traveled. Everything that participates in being in road one, and everything that participates in truth in road two, all derive their integrity as participations in the ultimate being and the ultimate truth both of which are the one and the same God.

---

[114] MacIntyre. 122.

Let us consider as a proposition of first philosophy that all creation is actuated by love. In order to make discussion of this idea of love more accessible to a philosophy of realism I will speak of it as relation. The relation I have in mind is ultimately love, however, philosophy and love lack a common language so to discuss love philosophically, or philosophy from a standpoint of love, would handicap them both. Moreover, my purpose is not so much to elaborate a theory as to consider some of the twentieth century initiatives that relate to the proposal of relation as a philosophical principle. We will look at one line of defense against this idea, and three lines advancing the idea. The defender of an undisturbed Christian metaphysics of being is Jacques Maritain. The proponents of a Christian metaphysics of relation are Gabriel Marcel, Karol Wojtyla or John Paul II and, in a creative response to Wojtyla, W. Norris Clarke, S.J.

Philosophy grounded in being usually provides some sort of easement or special case status for the transcendent. Beauty, art, music and all the affectivities of our experience resist being reduced, cognized, or rendered intelligible by road one, which is given to causality, teleology, and predication. In the transcendent something different is going on that is more mysterious.

JACQUES MARITAIN

Jacques Maritain is an example of a twentieth century Thomist whose ontology of being brooks no compromise with affectivity. Intelligibility is being and being is intelligibility. At the summit of knowledge is the intuition of pure being. Being is superabundant, trans-formal, trans-essential, transcendent, super-intelligible and at the core of everything. As I understand Maritain's conception, being, either by analogy or in its pure form as an ideating ontological intuition, is the coin of all knowledge and experience. In the following citation from the third lecture of his Preface to Metaphysics Maritain enthuses about the boundary experience that distinguishes the metaphysician:

On the other hand, as I have just said, such experiences bring us to the threshold which it is then for us to cross by taking the decisive step. We do this by letting the veils —too heavy with matter and too opaque—of the concrete psychological or ethical fact fall away to discover in their purity the strictly metaphysical values which such experiences concealed. There is then but one word by which we can express our discovery, namely being. Let us have the courage to require our intellect, acting as such, to look the reality signified by the term in the face. It is something primordial, at once very simple and very rich and, if you will, inexpressible in the sense that it is that whose perception is the most difficult to describe, because it is the most immediate. Here we are at the root, at last laid bare, of our entire intellectual life.[115]

We shall return to Maritain to see how he responds to a proposal of Gabriel Marcel.

GABRIEL MARCEL

The ontology of Gabriel Marcel leaves more room for the affective, mysterious and transcendent, and seems to make them more accessible, cognizable and intelligible than the metaphysics of Saint Thomas as mediated by Maritain. This is very interesting because facile openness to mystery and the transcendent is desirable for an ontology that would give pride of place to relation over being. Marcel takes up these notions of mystery, transcendence and relation head-on. He proposes an understanding of mystery that is helpful. First, he proposed that our knowledge of ordinary things is gained by problem solving by which we

---

[115] Jacques Maritain, *A Preface to Metaphysics: Seven Lectures on Being* (New York: Sheed & Ward, 1948). 52-53

objectify the thing under consideration and apply appropriate objective criteria to its analysis. However, when we ourselves are involved as part of the data that is under consideration, mystery enters into the picture and objectification is no longer possible. When we are involved objectivity, our objectification, is adulterated by subjectivity. We can think of characteristics of subjectivity such as interiority, incommunicability, irreducibility and inter-subjectivity. All these influences and more are integral to the makeup of the thinking subject who presumes to objectify or be objective about himself. Therefore, even though he may think he is in the realm of problem solving, he is really in the realm of the meta-problematical, or, the realm of mystery. The self-understanding of the human person is not objective nor can it be objectified. A strategy that tries to objectify mystery and apply appropriate objective criteria will miss the mark. The mysterious requires us to recognize this limitation on our ability to reduce phenomena to categories.

Consider these excerpts from his essay, *The Ontological Mystery*:

> A mystery is a problem which encroaches upon its own data, invading them as it were, and thereby transcending itself as a simple problem.... It will be seen at once that there is no hope of establishing an exact frontier between problem and mystery. For in reflecting on a mystery we tend inevitably to degrade it to the level of a problem[116]

Having so defined the frontier between a problem and a meta-problem, or mystery, and having made clear that the frontier cannot be established exactly, Marcel uses the unity of body and soul as an example of a mystery we cannot stand alongside and solve as a problem. However, he goes on to explain that in the face of another mystery the frontier itself vanishes:

---

[116] Gabriel Marcel, *The Philosophy of Existentialism* (New York: The Citadel Press, 2002). 19

But it is, of course, in love that the obliteration of this frontier can best be seen. It might perhaps even be shown that the domain of the meta-problematical coincides with that of love, and that love is the only starting point for the understanding of such mysteries as that of the body and soul, which, in some manner, is its expression. [117]

Further on he assigns an ontological value to an aspect of love that is relational and of interest to our exploration.

It will be asked: What is the criterion of true love? It must be answered that there is no criteriology except in the order of the objective and the problematical; but we can already see at a distance the eminent ontological value to be assigned to fidelity.[118]

By this last citation it is to be understood that the idea of applying appropriate objective criteria makes no sense in the realm of mystery, and that further there is an ontological character to fidelity which is a manifestation of love.

It is on this point that Maritain takes issue with Marcel. If I understand him correctly, for Maritain, fidelity does not have an ontological value but is instead an affectivity that properly falls under the criterion of being, -just as everything else does. Here is Maritain reading of Marcel's point:

It would seem that M. Gabriel Marcel is seeking a method of approach to metaphysical being by deepening the sense of certain moral facts such as fidelity.... the notion of fidelity is here understood in a sense which does or should transcend ethics and conveys strictly metaphysical value and content. ...Therefore, if I rightly understand M. Marcel's

---

[117] Ibid. 20
[118] Ibid.

thought, if we follow its direction, we shall conclude that a philosophy of life which confuses my *self* with the flux of my life is inconsistent with the experience of fidelity. The experience, the irreducible reality of what I experience and know as fidelity, is pregnant with an ontological realism.[119]

In Maritain's gracious but dismissive response to Marcel he claims that fidelity:

> ...belongs to the practical and moral order, the psychological factor being invested with the ethical. If we stop here, I maintain we have not crossed the threshold of metaphysics. These explorations...can provide a most valuable service...but only if we travel further; cross the threshold, take the decisive step. [120]

Maritain's description of the decisive step across the threshold has already been quoted. So, we have an example of two views of where a threshold into the realm of ontology may be located. From our discussion of MacIntyre's analysis of Thomistic foundations, Maritain seems to claim that road one is the only road open for philosophy to get to the ultimate ontological reality of superabundant being by way of an intuition of being. Marcel seems to claim that road two is open for philosophy to get to the ultimate metaphysical reality of love, in this case love and fidelity, by way of an intuition of truth. These are examples of two contrasting views in twentieth century Christian ontology. Maritain is a disciple of Aquinas whereas Marcel is not. Marcel is a phenomenologist whereas Maritain is not. The heart of the matter brings to light a crisis of confidence in the ability of a Thomistic ontology of being to provide an adequate account of the human person.

---

[119] Maritain. 50
[120] Ibid. 51

KAROL WOJTYLA

In a paper entitled *Subjectivity and the Irreducible in the Human Being*, Karol Wojtyla expressed the view that the metaphysics that came from Aristotle through the Scholastics to Descartes had not presented a balanced anthropology of the human person because it did not adequately consider the unique and irreducible lived experience of each human person. The paper was sent to an international conference held in Paris in June of 1975, and key excerpts follow and are repeated as appropriate in other sections of the thesis dissertation:

> The experience of the human being cannot be derived by way of cosmological reduction; we must pause at the irreducible, at that which is unique and unrepeatable in each human being, by virtue of which he or she is not just *a particular human being*—an individual of a certain species—but a *personal subject*. Only then do we get a true and complete picture of the human being.[121]

Moreover, access to the irreducible in the individual human person is closed to a reductive method, for example, to genus and species, and open to an inductive method like phenomenology.

> The irreducible signifies that which is essentially incapable of reduction, that which cannot be reduced but can only be *disclosed* or *revealed*. *Lived experience essentially defies reduction*. This does not mean however that it eludes knowledge; it only means that we must arrive at the knowledge of it differently, namely by a method or means of analysis that merely reveals and discloses

---

[121] Karol Wojtyla, "Subjectivity and the Irreducible in the Human Being," in *Catholic Thought from Lublin: Person and Community*, ed. Andrew N. Woznicki (New York: Peter Lang, 1993).

its essence. The method of phenomenological analysis allows us to pause at lived experience as the irreducible.... Phenomenological analysis thus contributes to trans-phenomenal understanding;[122]

W. NORRIS CLARKE, S.J

In response to Karol Wojtyla's identification of the need, the opportunity and the means of complementing Thomistic metaphysics with the "distinct new phenomenology of Christian Personalism," Clarke has taken a further step "by showing how a personalistic dimension is actually implicit within the very structure and meaning of being itself in a fully developed Thomistic metaphysics..."[123] In agreement with Wojtyla that the objective structures of metaphysics cannot adequately account for the irreducible, and that that lived experience requires inductive phenomenological analysis, (a meta-problematic analysis in Marcel's account), Clarke shows how it all fits together. He identifies the structures in Thomistic ontology that contain their own warrant for further elaboration. He locates the interiority of existing things in their act of existing, which is, in standard Thomistic ontology, an act of existing according to the kind of the existent in act. However, the act of existence, according to genus and species or kind, is an act of outward communication of the existent to the whole community of beings. All communication is both given by the community of beings and received by the community of beings. In the case of the human person the act of existence is not reducible to its kind, genus and species, but unique and unrepeatable in each individual person. Moreover, its uniqueness is

---

[122] ibid. 215-6
[123] Norris W. Clarke, S.J., "The Integration of Personalism and Thomistic Metaphysics in 21ˢᵗ Century Thomism," in *The Creative Retrieval of Saint Thomas Aquinas: Essays in Thomistic Philosophy, New and Old* (New York: Fordham University Press 2009).

largely accounted for by the life experience of the individual and so is only accessible through inductive, phenomenological analysis. This dimension of the human person is essential for anthropology and ethics. At length Clarke describes the assist Revelation gives to this phenomenon, in the mystery of the Blessed Trinity, a one in being community of persons.

To sum up, MacIntyre, a twentieth century philosopher and Thomist, characterized Saint Thomas as offering us two roads, being and truth, to the same metaphysical destination, God. We considered a twentieth century Christian metaphysician, Jacques Maritain, a Thomist, for whom the first principle of first philosophy was being, and for whom every philosophical question was ultimately reducible to being. Then we considered a twentieth century Christian metaphysician, Gabriel Marcel, a phenomenologist and not a Thomist. Marcel seemed to say that the second road, the road of truth leading to the same destination, could be plied by the meta-problematic, which are mysteries, like love and fidelity. We acknowledged Karol Wojtyla, a twentieth century Christian metaphysician Thomist, student of phenomenology, Pope and saint, who claimed that Aristotelian, Scholastic and Cartesian ontology up to the present has been inadequate to fully explain the human person anthropologically, and hence, from the standpoint of ethics. Finally, we considered W. Norris Clarke, S.J., a twentieth century Christian metaphysician and Thomist who took up Wojtyla's challenge and showed how and where the personalism in need of phenomenological elaboration were already to a degree implicit in the ontology of Thomas Aquinas.

Christian metaphysicians were driven back to the drawing boards by historical contingencies of the twentieth century. Two major historical phenomena fell into the first half and the second half of the twentieth century. The first half accumulated a horrific body count through war, genocide and totalitarianism that is unique in all of history. The second half embraced a contraceptive mentality that hollowed out traditional cultures, and adopted a back-up strategy of abortion in case contraception failed, that stacked up an even greater body count, and imploded Western populations. The first half problem apparently has peaked, for now, but the second half problem is insidious and is gaining steam. In dealing with these problems all roads lead to ethics, from which all roads lead to anthropology, from which all roads lead to metaphysics.

The *Theology of the Body* aims precisely at remedying a failed pastoral initiative, -the encyclical *Humanae Vitae*, which was handicapped by an inadequate theological anthropology. That anthropology applies objective criteria to define man in categories of genus and species that are congenial to cosmological reduction and to an ontology of being. However, these are precisely the philosophical tools phenomenologists and personalists insist are inimical to an adequate account of human beings. The *Theology of the Body* aims precisely at completing this anthropology by applying subjective criteria which require different philosophical tools to reach the experience of subjectivity in each human person. These tools are inductive rather than deductive and phenomenological rather than categorical. These are the analytical tools of the *Theology of the Body*. They are applied to what scripture discloses about our first parents' experience of subjectivity. By re-connecting the Christian mystery of creation to the subjectivity of man through the experience of our first parents, the *Theology of the Body* proposes a more complete and adequate theological anthropology. This more adequate anthropology develops an otherwise static anthropology and a sterile ethical analysis that led to the pastoral failure of *Humanae Vitae* and accelerated a culture of death.

This method of identifying what scripture discloses opens new horizons for theological anthropology and ethics by opening a new horizon for a better understanding of conjugal love. For the above reasons, this dissertation accepts that rigorously undertaken phenomenological subjective and inductive analysis is a solid philosophical basis for scriptural exegeses that can lead to sound theological articulation, and potentially doctrinal development.

Of the two roads for first philosophy to travel to get to the same place, I believe John Paul's *Theology of the Body* travels the length of road two and reaches its destination, the God of Being, Truth and Love. Aided by the Revelation of the Blessed Trinity, we know this God is a community of love. When we look into His face we will be impressed by His essence and existence; we will admire His truth but His love will act upon us. Reality will be recognized as analogous to the mutual self-gift of nuptial love, spawning being in truth, as is communicated by our bodies, by the Revelation of creation, by the Blessed Trinity, by the Paschal mystery. It is no less real for being symbolic. In filiation and spiration love trumps being and accounts for it. Love brings being into being nuptially in the dimension of gift. In a *Theology of the Body* footnote, on the referring to scriptural exegesis John Paul II commented: "The question, whether the metaphysical reduction really expresses the content which the symbolical and metaphorical language conceals within itself, is another matter."[124]

Having considered the *bona fides* of philosophizing according to *De Veritatae* and according to *De Ente et Essentia*, Part I.5 will consider the degree of papal authority that attaches to *Humanae Vitae* and to the *Theology of the Body* as two papal pronouncements.

I.5 Authority of Papal Pronouncements

Regarding the authority of *Humanae Vitae*, an encyclical, and the *Theology of the Body*, a catechesis, both are papal pronouncements, both belong to the ordinary magisterium of the Church, and both are to be adhered to by the faithful with religious assent. However, papal encyclicals as a form of teaching carry greater doctrinal weight and authority than less formal pronouncements such as catecheses delivered to informal papal audiences.

Therefore, *Humanae Vitae* as an encyclical, carries greater doctrinal weight than the *Theology of the Body*, a catechesis. However, *Humanae Vitae's* authority exceeds the authority due to it because of its form as an encyclical. *Humanae Vitae* is an encyclical that constitutes a definitive action on the part of the Roman Pontiff, as head of the college of bishops and supreme pastor and teacher of all the faithful, proclaiming and

---

[124] John Paul II, *Man and Woman He Created Them; a Theology of the Body*. Footnote, 141.

affirming a constant moral doctrine of the Church, such that in virtue of his office it enjoys the infallibility promised to the Church. Consequently, *Humanae Vitae* binds the faithful to adhere to its doctrine with the assent of faith. The Catechism of the Catholic Church explains:

> The Roman Pontiff, head of the college of bishops, enjoys this infallibility in virtue of his office, when, as supreme pastor and teacher of all the faithful—who confirms his brethren in the faith— he proclaims by a definitive act a doctrine pertaining to faith or morals. . .. The infallibility promised to the Church is also present in the body of bishops when, together with Peter's successor, they exercise the supreme Magisterium, above all in an Ecumenical Council. [418 LG 25; cf. Vatican Council I: DS 3074.] (CCC 891)

Therefore, the moral prohibition of contraception is authoritatively and infallibly proclaimed by the encyclical *Humanae Vitae* and carries maximal doctrinal authority.

What then is the authority of the *Theology of the Body*? The *Theology of the Body* seeks to deepen the explanation for the moral doctrine proclaimed by *Humanae Vitae*. For example, as pursued by this thesis, the *Theology of the Body* proclaims a further inference, viz. that anthropologically, the holiness of the conjugal act, understood in a micro sense as the one-flesh union of husband and wife, and understood in a macro sense as marriage, is the foundation of the sacramental order (TOB 95b.7,2) and the order of grace (TOB 95b.4). If this thesis is correct that this inference is what the *Theology of the Body* teaches, the faithful would be bound to adhere to it with religious assent, which is less binding than being bound by the assent of faith, but is nonetheless an extension of the assent of faith that is compelled by the encyclical *Humanae Vitae*. This inference, however, would not enjoy the authoritative doctrinal weight of infallibility, unless and until it were to be proclaimed to be an article of faith in like manner to the proclamation of *Humanae Vitae's* moral proclamation. As a papal catechetical teaching, the *Theology of the Body* itself, and its inferences, do not enjoy the doctrinal weight of papal infallibility. This is because the catechesis is not a definitive act, does not provide a doctrinal definition, and is not pronounced or proclaimed by the Roman Pontiff in a definitive manner as is the moral doctrine of *Humanae Vitae*. Again, the Catechism of the Catholic Church explains:

> Divine assistance is also given to the successors of the apostles, teaching in communion with the successor of Peter, and, in a particular way, to the bishop of Rome, pastor of the whole Church, when, without arriving at an infallible definition and without pronouncing in a "definitive manner," they propose in the exercise of the ordinary Magisterium a teaching that leads to better understanding of Revelation in matters of faith and morals. To this ordinary teaching the faithful "are to adhere to it with religious assent" which, though distinct from the assent of faith, is nonetheless an extension of it. (CCC 892)

Accordingly, the *Theology of the Body* is a catechesis that, without arriving at an infallible definition and without pronouncing in a 'definitive manner,' nevertheless proposes a teaching that leads to better understanding of Revelation in matters of faith and morals. It is exercised with divine assistance, in a particular way, coming as it does from the bishop of Rome, pastor of the whole Church, and the faithful are to adhere to it with religious assent as an extension of the deposit of faith.

To the extent that the *Theology of the Body* affirms the moral teaching of *Humanae Vitae*, the faithful are to adhere to its teaching with the assent of faith or as an extension of the deposit of faith. However, my thesis stops short claiming that inferences found in the *Theology of the Body* such as; 'anthropologically, the conjugal act is the foundation of the sacramental order and the order of grace,' are comparably compelling. On the other hand, the faithful are to accord religious assent to validly drawn inferences as extensions of the deposit of faith. At present the inference said to be drawn by this thesis cannot be called a genuine doctrinal development. However, the thesis shows that at some future time it may be taught as such and that it is not disqualified as a potential genuine doctrinal development by application of the criteria supplied by Newman. In any case, as an inference drawn by the *Theology of the Body* it is, on its face, an opening to a new horizon for theological anthropology and the theology of marriage.

To summarize, *Humanae Vitae* as an encyclical carries greater authority than the *Theology of the Body* as a catechesis. In addition, this particular encyclical meets the requirements of an authoritatively and infallibly proclaimed moral doctrine. The *Theology of the Body* proclaims a further inference, viz. that the holiness of conjugal love is the foundation of the sacramental order and the order of grace. This inference may be true, but it does not enjoy the same authoritative, infallible or doctrinal weight as *Humanae Vitae's* moral doctrine because it does not arrive at an infallible definition, and is not pronounced in a definitive manner.

Nevertheless, this thesis shows beyond reasonable doubt, that John Paul's *Theology of the Body* taught that conjugal love is the foundation of the sacramental order and the order of grace; that this inference is not easily dismissed as a potential genuine development of doctrine; and that, in any case, it opens a new theological horizon for theological anthropology and the theology of marriage.

Summary of Part I

Part I.1 surveyed speculative theological anthropologies from different Church Fathers, Doctors and saints. Part I.2 presented a contemporary articulation of natural law theory promulgated by the International Theological Commission with commentaries by noted theologians. Part I.3 presented Personalism as a philosophical movement and traced its origins to theology in Christianity's first centuries, to Ecumenical councils deliberating on Christological controversies, to the Old Testament Christian concept of creation *ex nihilo*, and to the understanding that orations and prophecies in the Old Testament were more than dramatic techniques but were actually the living God in dialog with his people. All these realities of Christianity bequeathed the concept of person to the ancient and modern world. Characteristics, examples and voices of personalism in philosophy and theology are briefly presented. Part I.4 entitled First Philosophy, contrasts an ontology of being with personalist ontology. Each uses different methods and both are valid paths to infinite Being and Truth. Part I.5 entitled Authority of Papal Pronouncements, concerns different levels of authority in different forms of Church teaching.

Part I's presentation of topics set the stage for Part II's formal comparison of *Humanae Vitae* and the *Theology of the Body* as two disparate theological genres. Having considered theological anthropology, natural law, personalism, the philosophical creditability of the *Theology of the Body's* methodology and inferences, and levels of papal authority in different forms of papal pronouncements, Part II proceeds to the analysis of the main argument. It compares the two documents; their goals, their different framing of questions, their different methodologies, the different authorities they invoke, and their different characterizations of the conjugal act. The doctrinal aspects of *Humanae Vitae* and the *Theology of the Body* are then presented in Part III. Analysis of doctrinal development relative to both documents is presented in Part IV. A summary of the dissertation, a conclusion and suggested topics for further study are presented in Part V.

+

PART II

Comparison between Humanae Vitae and the Theology of the Body

II.1 Introduction to Part II

Part II.1 first considers the historical relationship between the two teachings as explained in John Paul's final presentation of the *Theology of the Body*. Then it compares the two teachings in specific categories using pertinent texts from both documents. It compares the stated goals of *Humanae Vitae* and the stated goals of the *Theology of the Body*. Then it compares the way that *Humanae Vitae* and the *Theology of the Body* frame the theological questions to be pursued or answered in order to meet their respective goals. Next it compares the theological methodology and the authorities invoked by *Humanae Vitae* and the *Theology of the Body*. Then it compares the conjugal act as characterized by *Humanae Vitae* and by the *Theology of the Body*.

Part II.2 summarizes the differences between the *Theology of the Body* and *Humanae Vitae* from Part II.1 and clarifies how, in spite of these differences, the *Theology of the Body* is nevertheless in continuity with *Humanae Vitae* and develops its doctrine, or in Newman's phrase, brings aspects of the idea into consistency and form.

II.1a What is the Relationship between the *Theology of the Body* and *Humanae Vitae?*

As noted above, John Paul presented the *Theology of the Body* approximately eleven years after Pope Paul VI promulgated the encyclical *Humanae Vitae*. The *Theology of the Body* itself supports the thesis that it develops the doctrine of *Humanae Vitae*. The final presentation (TOB 133) explicitly connects the *Theology of the Body* in its entirety with *Humanae Vitae*.

John Paul said that all of the *Theology of the Body* should be understood as related to the doctrine of *Humanae Vitae*. He directly referenced Paul VI's expressed hope for a deeper theological explanation of *Humanae Vitae's* doctrine as the context in which the *Theology of the Body* is to be received. First, John Paul characterized both parts of the *Theology of the Body* (Part I, 'The Redemption of the Body;' and Part II, 'The Sacrament') as a commentary on *Humanae Vitae's* doctrine.[125] Second, he characterized all the *Theology of the Body* reflections as facing the important and difficult questions raised by *Humanae Vitae*.[126] Third, he reveals how the structure and method of the entire *Theology of the Body* begins and ends with *Humanae Vitae*. He points out that while he only directly raises the topic of *Humanae Vitae* in his final catecheses, he makes it clear that the entire *Theology of the Body* responds to the questions *Humanae Vitae* raised.[127]

---

[125] Ibid. "In some sense, one can say that all the reflections dealing with the "Redemption of the Body and the Sacramentality of Marriage" *seem* to constitute *an extensive commentary* on the doctrine contained precisely in *Humanae Vitae*." (TOB 133.2,3)

[126] Ibid. "The reflections carried out consist in facing the questions raised about *Humanae Vitae*. The reaction the encyclical stirred up confirms the importance and the difficulty of these questions. They are reaffirmed also by the further statements of Paul VI, where he emphasized the possibility of deepening the explanation of Christian truth in this area." (TOB 133.2,5)

[127] Ibid. "The catecheses devoted to *Humanae Vitae* constitute only one part, the final part, of those that dealt with the redemption of the body and the sacramentality of Marriage." (TOB 133.4,1) "If I draw particular attention precisely to these final

In this last citation John Paul also states that the final part of the *Theology of the Body* dealing with *Humanae Vitae* relates to the whole of the *Theology of the Body* homogeneously and organically. This explicitly acknowledges that the *Theology of the Body* and *Humanae Vitae* share the same root. The root doctrine of *Humanae Vitae* is that: "...each and every marriage act must remain open to the transmission of life." (HV 11). Both the *Theology of the Body* and *Humanae Vitae* are therefore teachings about the conjugal act. The *Theology of the Body* and *Humanae Vitae* are homogeneous and organically related because the single root of the two teachings is the conjugal act.

II.1b How do the Stated Goals of *Humanae Vitae* and the *Theology of the Body* Compare?

II.1b.i *Humanae Vitae:* Goals

What is the goal of *Humanae Vitae*? How does *Humanae Vitae* view its task, its *raison d'être*? What problem or problems does *Humanae Vitae* address?

Humanae Vitae's goal is to reaffirm the Church's moral teaching forbidding contraception in the context of contemporary demographic concerns and developments in fertility control technology. To paraphrase *Humanae Vitae*: society has evolved in ways that raise new questions concerning the most serious duty of the transmission of life; there are

---

catecheses, I do so not only because the topic discussed by them is more closely connected with our present age, but first of all *because it is from this topic that the questions spring* that run in some way through the whole of our reflections. It follows that this final part is not artificially added to the whole, but is organically and homogeneously united with it. In some sense, that part, which in the overall disposition is located at the end, is at the same time found at the beginning of the whole. This is important from the point of view of structure and method." (TOB 133.4,2)

questions of overpopulation and risks that authorities will mandate radical measures to address these threats; there is the challenge of providing housing and employment which exacerbates the difficulty of properly educating an elevated number of children; there are questions raised about the status of women in society; about the value of conjugal love in marriage; and about the meaning of conjugal acts in relation to that love. Above all, man's progress in dominating nature is seen to extend to his own total being, to the human body, to physical and social life, and even to the laws which regulate the transmission of life. Faced with these new questions, should ethical norms be revised? Should ethical norms govern overall fecundity rather than single conjugal acts? Should couples rely on their reason and will, rather than biological rhythms to regulate births? (HV 2-3)

Humanae Vitae seeks to proclaim anew the Church's moral teaching on contraception in light of the above questions in a contemporary secular ethos that views fertility control technologies to be a panacea for the abovementioned urgent socioeconomic challenges.

II.1b.ii *Theology of the Body:* Goals

What is the goal of the *Theology of the Body*? How does the *Theology of the Body* view its task, its *raison d'être*? What problem or problems does the *Theology of the Body* address?

The goal of the *Theology of the Body* is to face the important and the difficult questions raised about *Humanae Vitae* by deepening the explanation of Christian truth in this area. (*see* footnote 127, p. 97; TOB 133.2, 5). Given that it is "...*an extensive commentary* on the doctrine contained precisely in *Humanae Vitae*.," (see footnote 126, p 97; TOB 133.2, 3) and that the doctrine contained in *Humanae Vitae* is that: "... each and every marriage act must remain open to the transmission of life," (HV 11), the *Theology of the Body*'s goal is to deepen the explanation of Christian truth; specifically, the theological understanding of the conjugal act.

The chapter on Personalist Perspectives, (Part I.3.c) noted that Joseph Ratzinger criticized St. Augustine for the decisive mistake of proposing an inter-psychic analogy to explain the Blessed Trinity. The problem is twofold; first, the analogy reduces the Personal existences of the Blessed Trinity to essentialist or substantialist categories; and second, it crosses a line between substantial being and personal existence. Ratzinger complains that this analogy set Christian theological anthropology on a path of recognizing autonomous individual human psyches as representative of the Blessed Trinity and lost the sense of interpersonal community as proper to the image of God in man.

Ratzinger criticized St. Thomas for a similar defect. While Thomas proposed an existential, personalist, and communitarian theology of the Blessed Trinity he opted for a Boethian essentialist, substantialist, and naturalistic theological anthropology. Ratzinger's complaint is that Aquinas, like Augustine, crossed a line between personal existence and substantial being. Augustine could have been unaware of the boundary, but Aquinas would be aware of the boundary and crossed it anyway. We further noted that the *Theology of the Body* called for an adequate anthropology to remedy what Ratzinger called Augustine's decisive mistake and Aquinas' defect.

The *Theology of the Body's* remedy identifies the image of God the Blessed Trinity in human personhood as an existential category. As previously noted, our very idea of person comes from theology's meditation on the Blessed Trinity. We also noted that Richard of St. Victor identified personhood as an existential category rather than an essential or substantial category. To illustrate his point, he described God, angels and men as follows: in God, there is one substance and three Persons; in angels, there is one person and one substance; in man there is one person and more than one substance (spiritual and material). Richard defined the human person existentially as an incommunicably proper existence of a spiritual nature. Each person exists as an incommunicable subject, and each person shares an affinity of personhood with the Persons of the Blessed Trinity. Personhood, as incommunicable, is characterized by dominion and freedom. Dominion here is understood as dominion over oneself. Freedom is total discretion to exercise dominion by giving oneself over to the possession of another, and discretion to receive another's gift of his or her self as a possession. Put another way, persons are only communicable, that is, capable of being possessed by another, through the exercise of their dominion by free acts of giving and receiving. This insight of incommunicability is inaccessible to essentialist anthropologies that account for dominion and freedom as instrumental add-ons to a common substance. Therefore, giving and receiving can only be accounted for as instrumental to the common substance or nature, and in this understanding the substantial nature and its purposes serve as the ethical metric for human acts.

On the other hand, as an existential category, persons are constituted by their inherent capacity to exercise dominion and freedom in freely giving and freely receiving their otherwise incommunicable selves with others. According to this existential personalist anthropology, free acts of giving and receiving are not instrumental to a common nature, but constitutive of unique and unrepeatable personhood, that cannot be replicated. A communion of persons is formed by free acts of individual persons giving and receiving each other in all of their transcendent dignity. (see footnote 105, p. 69.) This free personal act of communion among persons shares affinity with the Communion of Persons that is the Blessed Trinity. And the free personal giving and receiving of the most intimate and total of human personal communions, expressed and realized in the one flesh union of man and wife, the conjugal act, is an image of the Blessed Trinity in man.

The above is an argument for why an anthropology based on an ontology of being and a deontological analysis of essential or substantial human nature, by itself, is less than an adequate foundation from which to fully explain the moral imperative of *Humanae Vitae*. It leaves aside the ontology of personhood and relies solely on the ontology of being, which is one perspective in which to understand Ratzinger's metaphor that we have built our closets too small.

When it came to the image of God in man, Augustine and Aquinas both operated under essentialist anthropologies. This, according to Ratzinger, accounts for Augustine's decisive mistake and Aquinas' defect. They were trapped, so to speak, in essentialist categories which, according to Ratzinger's metaphor, caused them to build their closets too small. They recognized human dominion and freedom as an essential rather than an existential category. They did not recognize existential incommunicability as an ontological ground of dominion and freedom. In the ethics of substantial freedom, the good comports with nature and its purposes. In the ethics of existential freedom, grounded in incommunicability, the good comports with giving and receiving gifts. Nature and purpose are substantialist criteria and gift giving and receiving are existentialist criteria. The freedom of the gift opens another dimension for ethical analysis. It also opens another dimension for analogies between God and man. Augustine locked an analogy to the Blessed Trinity within the individual human psyche. Aquinas rejected a family analogy to the Blessed Trinity on substantialist grounds: "this example from material origin seems to be a very poor choice to represent the immaterial procession of the Divine Persons."[128] By not operating in existential categories, and by limiting the affinities between divine and human persons to substantialist categories, Augustine and Aquinas failed to recognize the interpersonal giving and receiving of marriage and family as a communion analogous to the communion of the Blessed Trinity and an *imago Trinitatis*. Personalism, which transposes the concept of person from essential into existential categories, facilitates apprehension of those affinities not only as analogies but as icons, images, signs and sacraments.

---

[128] Aquinas, *Summa Theologica*.(ST, I.36.3.1)

II.1c How do *Humanae Vitae* and the *Theology of the Body* frame the questions they seek to answer?

II.1c.i *Humanae Vitae:* Framing the Question

Humanae Vitae frames the question it seeks to answer as a moral problematic brought into view by socioeconomic challenges and the progress of technology.

First, *Humanae Vitae* identifies human technological domination of nature as the source of the question to which the encyclical seeks to respond. Man is extending his reach beyond nature itself and into man's own total existence including his body, his physical and social existence, and even into the laws that regulate the transmission of life.[129] Second, this overreach requires the Church to reflect deeply on its moral teaching on marriage which is founded on natural law and divine revelation.[130] Third, it frames the question in terms of rights and duties of married couples.[131] Fourth, it refers the objective moral order to define the duties of the married couple,[132] and to the natural law, as interpreted by the constant teaching of the Church.[133] Having framed the question according to these parameters and authorities, the encyclical reasons to the moral imperative

---

[129] Paul VI, "…man's progress in dominating nature is being extended to his own total being, to the body, to physical and social life, and even to the laws which regulate the transmission of life." (HV 2)

[130] Ibid. "Such questions required of the Church a new and deeper reflection upon the principles of the moral teaching on marriage: a teaching founded on the natural law, illuminated and enriched by divine revelation." (HV 4)

[131] Ibid. "…a coherent teaching concerning both the nature of marriage and the correct use of conjugal rights and the duties of husband and wife." (HV 4)

[132] Ibid. "Responsible parenthood…concerns the objective moral order…keeping a right order of priorities, recognize…duties toward God, themselves, their families and human society" (HV 10)

[133] Ibid. "The Church calls men back to observance of the natural law, interpreted by its constant doctrine, that each and every marriage act must remain open to the transmission of life." (HV 11)

that: "each and every marriage act must remain open to the transmission of life"[134]

II.1c.ii *Theology of the Body:* Framing the Question

The *Theology of the Body* frames the question it seeks to answer as an anthropological problematic that calls for a deeper understanding of what scripture reveals about the human person and about the conjugal act.

The *Theology of the Body* responds to Paul VI's statements emphasizing the need to deepen the explanation of Christian truth in this area (*see* footnote 127, p., 97, TOB 133.2, 5). In addition, the *Theology of the Body* responds to the Apostolic Exhortation *Familiaris Consortio's* appeal to theologians concerning *Humanae Vitae*:

> For this reason, together with the Synod Fathers I feel it is my duty to extend a pressing invitation to theologians, asking them to unite their efforts in order to collaborate with the hierarchical Magisterium and to commit themselves to the task of illustrating ever more clearly the biblical foundations, the ethical grounds and the personalistic reasons behind this doctrine. (*FC* 31) [135]

Explicit appeals for scriptural, anthropological and personalistic analyses of the moral norm of *Humanae Vitae* are expressed repeatedly in the *Theology of the Body*, [136] and confirmed by the 1980 Synod on the Role

---

[134] Ibid.

[135] Pope John Paul II, "Familiaris Consortio," (Nov. 22, 1981 1981), accessed 2018, http://w2.vatican.va/content/john-paul-ii/en/apost_exhortations/documents/hf_jp-ii_exh_19811122_familiaris-consortio.html.#31

[136] John Paul II, *Man and Woman He Created Them; a Theology of the Body.* "The analysis of the personalistic aspects of the Church's teaching contained in Paul VI's encyclical highlights a resolute appeal to measure man's progress with the measure of the "person," that is, of that which is a good of man as man, which corresponds

of the Christian Family, *Familiaris Consortio*.[137] Therefore, emphasis on scripture, anthropology and the human person is the key to understanding the *Theology of the Body's* framing of the question in order to advance toward the goal of a deepening of our understanding of the Christian truth of the conjugal act, the subject of *Humanae Vitae's* moral doctrine.

---

to his essential dignity. (TOB 133.3,4), (*see also* footnote 116, TOB 133. 2, 5). "The analysis of the *personalistic aspects* leads to the conviction that the *fundamental problem* the encyclical presents is the viewpoint of *the authentic development of the human person*; such development should be measured, as a matter of principle, by the measure of ethics and not only "technology." (TOB 133.3,5). "The analysis of the *biblical aspects* speaks about the way of rooting the teaching proclaimed by the Church in revelation. This is important *for the development of theology*. Development or progress in theology takes place, in fact, through continually taking up again the study of the deposit of revelation." (TOB 133.3,1). "When the 'male' man, awakened from his Genesis sleep, says, 'This time she is flesh from my flesh and bone from my bones' (Gen. 2:23), these words in some way express the subjectively beatifying beginning of man's existence in the world. Inasmuch as this [expression of joy] was verified at the 'beginning,' it confirms the process of man's individuation in the world, and is born, so to speak, from the very depth of his human solitude, which he lives as a person in the face of all other creatures and all living beings (*animalia*). This 'beginning' too, belongs thus to an adequate anthropology and can always be verified based on that anthropology. This purely anthropological verification brings us, at the same time, to the topic of the 'person' and to the topic of 'body/sex.' This simultaneity is essential. In fact, if we dealt with sex without the person, this would destroy the whole adequacy of the anthropology that we find in Genesis." (TOB 14.3,1-2)

[137] Ibid."The exhortation *Familiaris Consortio*, fruit of the 1980 Synod of Bishops on "*De meneribus familiae christianae*, The Role [or Duties, Gifts, Tasks] of the Christian Family," confirms this. The document contains an appeal, addressed particularly to theologians, to work out more completely *the biblical and personalistic aspects of the doctrine* contained in *Humanae Vitae*." (TOB 133.2,6)

II.1d What methodologies and authorities are used by *Humanae Vitae* and the *Theology of the Body?*

II.1d.i *Humanae Vitae:* Methodology and Authority

Humanae Vitae's theological methodology is primarily an objective, deductive, deontological moral analysis based on an ontology or metaphysics of being and a Boethian anthropological understanding of man as a rational animal. It invokes the authority of natural aw,[138] divine law,[139] revelation and sacred tradition, understood as the constant teaching of the magisterium. Accordingly, its analyses consider the nature and purposes of the conjugal act[140], the meaning and value of the act,[141] the rights and duties of married couples,[142] and the demands of married love and responsible parenthood as these pertain to the conjugal act. It also invokes, in passing, the contemporary authority of the Second Vatican Council, citing *Gaudium et Spes'* self-discovery through the sincere gift of self.

In addition to deontological objective moral analysis, *Humanae Vitae's* methodology gives substantial weight to the authority of the constant moral teaching of the magisterium, the competence of the magisterium

---

[138] Paul VI, "Marriage and conjugal love are by their nature ordained toward the begetting and educating of children." (HV 9). "The Church calls men back to observance of the natural law, interpreted by her constant doctrine..." (HV 11).

[139] Ibid."...a true contradiction cannot exist between the divine laws pertaining to the transmission of life and those pertaining to the fostering of authentic conjugal love. (HV 24)

[140] Ibid."The transmission of human life is a most serious role in which married people collaborate freely and responsibly with God the Creator. (HV 1).

[141] Ibid. "...the value of conjugal love in marriage and the relationship of conjugal acts to this love." (HV 2)

[142] Ibid."... the nature of marriage, the correct use of conjugal rights, and the duties of spouses." (HV 4).

to interpret the natural law, [143] the divine will,[144] the sacramentality of marriage,[145] and the teachings of the Second Vatican Council.[146]

II.1d.ii *Theology of the Body:* Methodology and Authority

The *Theology of the Body's* theological methodology is primarily an anthropological exegesis, or analysis of scripture, in a predominantly phenomenological, subjective, experiential and personalist perspective:

> The analysis of the *biblical aspects* speaks about the way of rooting the teaching proclaimed by the Church in revelation. This is important *for the development of theology.* Development or progress in theology takes place, in fact, through continually taking up again the study of the deposit of revelation. (TOB 133.3,1)

The *Theology of the Body's* teaching is grounded in revelation and its analyses "of biblical aspects" begin with Christ's teaching on marriage and specifically with his response to the Pharisees' inquiry about the permissibility of divorce:

---

[143] Ibid. "No member of the faithful could possibly deny that the Church is competent in her magisterium to interpret the natural moral law. It is in fact indisputable... "(HV 4)

[144] Ibid. "God willed the inseparability of the two meanings, unitive and procreative, of the conjugal act." (HV 12)

[145] Ibid. "For baptized persons, moreover, marriage invests the dignity of a sacramental sign of grace, inasmuch as it represents the union of Christ and of the Church. (HV 8)

[146] Ibid. "By means of the reciprocal personal gift of self, proper and exclusive to them, husband and wife tend towards the communion of their beings in view of mutual personal perfection, to collaborate with God in the generation and education of new lives. (HV 8)

Have you not heard that from the beginning the Creator created them male and female and said 'For this reason a man will leave his father and mother and unite with his wife, and the two will be one flesh?' (Mt 19:3-8). (TOB 1.2)

With the authority contained in these words of Christ, the *Theology of the Body* unfolds the meanings of our anthropological rootedness in the one flesh union of man and woman, -the conjugal act. John Paul leaves no room for doubt that the one flesh union of man and wife of which Christ speaks is the conjugal act: "The unity about which Genesis 2:24 speaks ("and the two will be one flesh") is without doubt the unity that is expressed and realized in the conjugal act." (TOB 10.2)

Therefore, the *Theology of the Body's* development of the doctrine of *Humanae Vitae* begins on its first page where Christ refers to the original plan of God for the conjugal act, as the one flesh union of husband and wife, is made the subject and foundation of the *Theology of the Body's* anthropology. The root of the *Theology of the Body's* teaching and the root of *Humanae Vitae's* teaching is immediately established, on the first page so to speak, as one and the same, the conjugal act. Nevertheless, this relationship to *Humanae Vitae* will not be made explicit until many analyses later in the final part of the *Theology of the Body*.

The *Theology of the Body* proceeds to build its theological anthropology on the foundation of Christ's words about the original meaning of the conjugal act. John Paul's choice of texts will emphasize the subjective, experiential and personal dimensions of revelation's disclosures. He invokes the authority of scripture from the beginning as revealed in Genesis and employs the hermeneutics of gift and of person.

II.1d.ii.a *Theology of the Body:* Methodology - Hermeneutic of Gift

The *Theology of the Body* employs a hermeneutic of gift. It teaches us that although God created the world *ex nihilo*, the world was not a gift because there was not yet anyone to receive it. For the world to be a gift it must be received. To give a gift is a free act and to receive a gift is a free act. Both the act of giving a gift and the act of receiving a gift presuppose freedom. Adam differed from the rest of creation because God created Adam to be free. The *Theology of the Body* teaches that upon Adam's creation, the world became a gift because Adam was the first creature that was free and therefore capable of receiving the gift of the world.

Adam was created in the dimensions of freedom and gift. He is the one creature God created for his own sake.[147] Adam is himself a gift and Adam receives his existence as a gift. The rest of creation is also a gift given by God to Adam because Adam alone, being free, can receive the gift of the world.

The *Theology of the Body* traces Adam's experience in the beginning as he progresses from a situation of solitude to a situation of union to a situation of nakedness without shame. Initially, even though he is created in the dimension of gift and is in dialog with God and is made in the image of God and receives the world as a gift from God, Adam is nevertheless a solitary creature. That is because Adam has no peer with whom to "*make it possible to exist in a relation of reciprocal gift.*" (TOB 14.1). Adam has no one to whom he can give a gift. There is nothing he can give to God, and no other creature exists that is capable of receiving a gift.

Then, God created Eve and brought Eve to Adam who, on beholding Eve, abounds with joy. Eve is a gift to Adam who exclaims: "this at last is bone of my bone and flesh of my flesh." (Gen. 2:23) Adam and Eve are joyfully united in reciprocal gift and reception. Then the author of Genesis adds: "Therefore a man leaves his father and his mother and clings to his wife and they become one flesh. And the man and his wife were both naked, and were not ashamed." (Gen. 2:24-25). The *Theology of the*

---

[147] Pope Paul VI, "Gaudium Et Spes; the Pastoral Constitution on the Church in the Modern World," (1965), accessed 2018, http://www.vatican.va/archive/hist_councils/ii_vatican_council/documents/vat-ii_const_19651207_gaudium-et-spes_en.html.#24,3

Body explains this sequence of experiences, solitude-union-nakedness, in the dimension of gift:

> The dimension of gift is decisive for the essential truth and depth of the meaning of original solitude-union-nakedness. It stands also at the very heart of the mystery of creation, which allows us to build the theology of the body "from the beginning, but at the same time demands that we build it precisely in this way." (TOB 13.2,3)

In addition to standing at the heart of the mystery of creation from the very beginning and allowing us to build a theology of the body, it also provides an opening to the basis of an adequate anthropology:

> If the account of the creation of man in the two versions, that of Genesis 1 and the Yahwist version in Genesis 2, allows us to establish the original meaning of solitude, unity, and nakedness, by this very fact it also allows us to reach the basis of an adequate anthropology, which seeks to understand and interpret man in what is essentially human. (TOB 13.2,1)

Moreover, in addition to allowing us to build a theology the body and an adequate anthropology, it authorizes us to understand that the body bears the divine image, the *imago Dei*, as two ways of being a body:

> Man, whom God created "male and female," bears the divine image impressed in the body "from the beginning"; man and woman constitute, so to speak, two diverse ways of "being a body" that are proper to human nature in the unity of this image.
> (TOB 13.2,2)

When John Paul speaks of the dimension of gift he gives us to understand that the human body male and female, masculine and feminine, was not simply created but was also given to us to be a visible sign in the world of the invisible divine Communion of Persons, the Communion of Truth and Love, which is the Blessed Trinity.

Man, male and female, could only be a sign of the divine Communion of Persons, the Blessed Trinity, if man, male and female, were free, since freedom is requisite to gift giving and receiving. Hence, God communicates Himself to man in the dimension of gift as a visible and efficacious sign of the immanent and economic Blessed Trinity by constituting us in freedom as male and female. Put another way, man, male and female, is a primordial sacrament of the relation of Persons within the Blessed Trinity, in addition to being a prophetic sign of the relations between God and Israel, and between Christ and the Church. Because this gift is transmitted into the world as freedom, and is visibly manifest by the body, man, male and female, is capacitated for reciprocal self-gift, and by this capacity, is enabled to be holy. Holiness entered the world as the capacity for self-gift. John Paul expresses this thought as follows:

> ...through the whole depth of their anthropological meaning, the words of Genesis 2:25 ("Both were naked, the man and his wife, but they did not feel shame") express the fact that, *together with man, holiness has entered the visible world,* the world created for him. The sacrament of the world, and the sacrament of man in the world, comes forth from the divine source of holiness and is instituted, at the same time, for holiness. Original innocence, connected with the experience of the spousal meaning of the body, is holiness itself, which permits man to express himself deeply with his own body, precisely through the "sincere gift" of self [*Gaudium et Spes,* 24:3]. Consciousness of the gift conditions in this case "the

sacrament of the body': in his body as man and woman, man senses himself as a subject of holiness. (TOB 19:5)

Having identified this primordial, pre-historical, and pre-lapsarian situation of solitude, union, and nakedness without shame, to be our original anthropology, the *Theology of the Body* develops this anthropology in the context of the first covenant between God and Adam. Thereafter, when Adam breaks the covenant by eating the forbidden fruit, the original anthropology is ruptured and lapsarian history begins.

II.1d.ii.b *Theology of the Body:* Methodology – Hermeneutic of Person

In the *Theology of the Body* John Paul identifies the fundamental viewpoint of *Humanae Vitae* to be its focus on the authentic development of the human person and not only a question of technological development:

> The analysis of the *personalistic aspects* leads to the conviction that the *fundamental problem* the encyclical [*Humanae Vitae*] presents is the viewpoint of *the authentic development of the human person*; such development should be measured, as a matter of principle, by the measure of ethics and not only "technology." (TOB 133.3,5)

In the *Theology of the Body* the free, reciprocal self-giving of Adam and Eve, represented in the experience of original nakedness without shame, because it is free, calls for criteria of personalism rather than criteria of naturalism. Here John Paul teaches us that the freedom to give and receive does not belong to the nature or substance or essence of man, but rather to his existential subjectivity or his person, which alone, and incommunicably, possesses the freedom of the gift. This, in turn, calls for a hermeneutic of person, which opens the horizon of a 'communion of persons' in the image of God. (Gen. 1:27). The *Theology of the Body* expresses this clearly:

> The whole biblical narrative and particularly the Yahwist text, shows that, through its own visibility, the body *manifests* man and, in manifesting him, acts as an intermediary that allows man and woman, from the beginning, to "communicate" with each other according to that *communio personarum* willed for them in particular by the Creator. Only this dimension, it seems, allows us to understand rightly the meaning of original nakedness. In this context, any "naturalistic" criterion is bound to fail, while the "personalistic" criterion can be of great help. (TOB 12.4,5)

Having established the inadequacy of naturalistic criteria and a requirement for personalistic criteria, the *Theology of the Body* applies the criteria to the one flesh union of man and wife to deepen the understanding of the communion of persons effected by the conjugal act:

> The unity about which Genesis 2:24 speaks ("and the two will be one flesh") is without doubt the unity that is expressed and realized in the conjugal act. The biblical formulation, so extremely concise and simple, indicates sex, that is, masculinity and femininity, as the characteristic of man —male and female- that allows them, when they become one flesh, to place their whole humanity at the same time under the blessing of fruitfulness. Yet, the whole context of the lapidary formulation does not allow us to stop on the surface of human sexuality; it does not allow us to treat the body and sex outside the full dimension of man and the "communion of persons," but imposes on us from

the "beginning" the obligation to see the fullness and depth proper to this unity that man and woman must constitute in the light of the revelation of the body. (TOB 10.2,1)

Having concluded that the whole context of Genesis 2:24 does not allow us to stop on the surface of human sexuality, which I understand to mean to stop at a naturalistic level, John Paul takes a further step by identifying the communion of persons of the conjugal act with the image of God the Blessed Trinity, the *imago Dei*:

Genesis 2:25 certainly speaks of something extraordinary that lies outside the limits of shame known by human experience and that is *decisive for the particular experience of interpersonal communication*, for the fullness that is rooted in the very heart of the *communio* revealed and developed in this way. In such a relationship the words "they did not feel shame" can only signify (*in sensu obliquo* [in an indirect sense]) an original depth in affirming what is inherent in the person, that is, what is "visibly" feminine and masculine, through which the "personal intimacy" of reciprocal communication is constituted in all its radical simplicity and purity. To this fullness of "*exterior perception*" expressed by physical nakedness, corresponds the "*interior*" *fullness of the vision of man in God*, that is, *according to the measure of the "image of God"* (see Gen. 1:27). (TOB 12.5)

Only personalist criteria make it possible for an exegesis to reach the depths implied in the interpersonal communion realized in the conjugal act. The same affinities could not be reached by cosmological reduction or naturalistic, essentialist or substantialist criteria. Hence, a personalistic hermeneutic is required with personalistic criteria.

II.1e How do *Humanae Vitae* and the *Theology of the Body* characterize the conjugal act?

II.1e.i *Humanae Vitae:* Characterization of the Conjugal Act

Humanae Vitae and the *Theology of the Body* both understand the conjugal act as sexual intercourse between husband and wife. Nevertheless, characterization of the conjugal act is different in the two teachings.

Humanae Vitae characterizes the conjugal act in categories that facilitate *Humanae Vitae's* moral analysis. So, the conjugal act is spoken of in terms of natural and divine law, according to its natural ends, purposes, or meanings, and according to the divine will and man's vocation.

For example, the encyclical speaks of the vocation to marriage as a role in which couples collaborate with God in his Creation: "The transmission of human life is a most serious role in which married people collaborate freely and responsibly with God the Creator." (HV 1). It speaks of marriage as being ordered by nature to the procreation and education of children: "Marriage and conjugal love are by their nature ordained toward the begetting and educating of children." (HV 9). It speaks of conjugal acts relative to the love between the married couple: "...the value of conjugal love in marriage and the relationship of conjugal acts to this love." (HV 2). It speaks in terms of nature, rights and duties, "... the nature of marriage, the correct use of conjugal rights, and the duties of spouses." (HV 4). It speaks in terms of the correct regulation of births, "Its task [the preparatory study commission] was to examine views and opinions concerning married life, and especially on the correct regulation of births;" (HV 5). It speaks in terms of the compatibility between the divine law and authentic love, "...a true contradiction cannot exist between the divine laws pertaining to the transmission of life and those pertaining to the fostering of authentic conjugal love" (HV 24).

In addition to describing the conjugal act in terms congenial to naturalistic deontological moral analysis, *Humanae Vitae* emphasizes the authority of tradition, the competence of the magisterium, the constancy of the Church's moral teaching including Second Vatican Council formulations, the natural law, the divine will for marriage, and its sacramentality.

For example, the encyclical speaks of the competence of the magisterium: "No member of the faithful could possibly deny that the Church is competent in her magisterium to interpret the natural moral law. It is in fact indisputable..." (HV 4). It speaks of the position of prominence of the natural law as the doctrine of the Church: "The Church calls men back to observance of the natural law, interpreted by its constant doctrine..." (HV 11). It speaks of the will of God: "God willed the inseparability of the two meanings, unitive and procreative, of the conjugal act." (HV 12) It connects the marriage of the baptized with the dignity of a sacramental sign of the relationship between Christ and the Church: "For baptized persons, moreover, marriage invests the dignity of a sacramental sign of grace, inasmuch as it represents the union of Christ and of the Church." (HV 8). The encyclical references personal self-gift and communion leading to mutual perfection of the spouses through their collaboration with God: "By means of the reciprocal personal gift of self, proper and exclusive to them, husband and wife tend towards the communion of their beings in view of mutual personal perfection, to collaborate with God in the generation and education of new lives." (HV 8).

This last reference to reciprocal self-gift and communion of beings, is not developed in *Humanae Vitae* and awaits the *Theology of the Body* for its development.

II.1e.ii *Theology of the Body:* Characterization of the Conjugal Act

The *Theology of the Body* characterizes the conjugal act as an image of the Blessed Trinity. This greatly develops *Humanae Vitae's* last referenced characterization: "the reciprocal personal gift of self, proper and exclusive to them," by means of which "husband and wife tend towards the communion of their beings in view of mutual personal perfection, to collaborate with God in the generation and education of new lives." (HV 8)

The *Theology of the Body* deepens this theological understanding by changing "the communion of their beings," a metaphysical or natural criterion and characterization, to "the communion of their persons," which is a personalistic criterion and characterization. The pivot from a "naturalistic" to a "personalistic" analysis is critical to the *Theology of the Body's* development of *Humanae Vitae's* doctrine because it opens *Humanae Vitae's* teaching to a different and deeper anthropological foundation, and to a different and deeper mystical context. The key pivotal passage(s) quoted under the 'Hermeneutic of Person' above, presuming the patience of the reader, is repeated here for convenience and emphasis:

> The whole biblical narrative and particularly the Yahwist text, shows that, through its own visibility, the body *manifests* man and, in manifesting him, acts as an intermediary that allows man and woman, from the beginning, to "communicate" with each other according to that *communio personarum* willed for them in particular by the Creator. Only this dimension, it seems, allows us to understand rightly the meaning of original nakedness. In this context, any "naturalistic" criterion is bound to fail, while the "personalistic" criterion can be of great help. (TOB 12.5)

The other key pivotal passage quoted under the 'Hermeneutic of Person' above also warrants repeating for clarity and emphasis. It is the passage in the *Theology of the Body* concretizing the conjugal act in the personalistic context of a communion of persons in mutual self-gift under the blessing of fruitfulness:

90

The unity about which Genesis 2:24 speaks ("and the two will be one flesh") is without doubt the unity that is expressed and realized in the conjugal act. The biblical formulation, so extremely concise and simple, indicates sex, that is, masculinity and femininity, as the characteristic of man –male and female- that allows them, when they become one flesh, to place their whole humanity at the same time under the blessing of fruitfulness. Yet, the whole context of the lapidary formulation does not allow us to stop on the surface of human sexuality; it does not allow us to treat the body and sex outside the full dimension of man and the "communion of persons," but imposes on us from the "beginning" the obligation to see the fullness and depth proper to this unity that man and woman must constitute in the light of the revelation of the body. (TOB 10.2,1)

What is the fullness and depth proper to this unity that man and woman must constitute that these reflections oblige us to see from the beginning? The fullness and depth of the one flesh union of man and woman, the conjugal act, is characterized explicitly as the image of God, the Blessed Trinity:

The account of the Creation of man in Genesis:1, affirms from the beginning and directly that man was created in the image of God inasmuch as he is male and female. The account in Genesis:2 by contrast, does not speak of the "image of God," but reveals, in the manner proper to it, that the complete and definitive creation of "man" (subject first to the experience of original solitude) expresses itself in giving life to the "communion personarum" that man and woman form. In this way the Yahwist agrees with the content of the first account. If, vice versa, we want to retrieve also from the account of the Yahwist text the concept of "image of God," we can deduce that *man became the image of God not only through his own humanity, but also through the communion of persons,* which man and woman form from the very beginning. The function of the image is that of mirroring the one who is the model, of reproducing its own prototype. Man becomes the image of God not so much in the moment of solitude as in the moment of communion. He is, in fact, from "the beginning' not only an image in which the solitude of one Person, who rules the world, mirrors itself, but also and essentially the image of an inscrutable divine communion of Persons. (TOB 9.3)

First, the *Theology of the Body* establishes the need for personalistic criteria: "...any "naturalistic" criterion is bound to fail, while the "personalistic" criterion can be of great help." Second, it characterizes the conjugal act, such that it "allows them, when they become one flesh, to place their whole humanity at the same time under the blessing of fruitfulness," as a "communion of persons" in mutual self-gift. Third, the communion of persons is characterized as an image of the Communion of Persons that is the Blessed Trinity. In this way, the *Theology of the Body* characterizes the conjugal act as the image of God the Blessed Trinity.

Summary of Part II

John Paul tells us in the final part of the *Theology of the Body* which reflects on *Humanae Vitae* that the whole of the *Theology of the Body* reflects on *Humanae Vitae* homogeneously and organically. To be homogeneously and organically related is, if not explicit recognition, at least an implicit recognition that both teachings have a common root. The subject matter of *Humanae Vitae* is the conjugal act and its doctrinal root is the moral imperative that: "...each and every marriage act must remain open to the transmission of life (HV 11)." To be organically and homogeneously related to *Humanae Vitae* implies, if not explicitly acknowledges, that the subject matter of the *Theology of the Body* is the conjugal act.

The goal of *Humanae Vitae* is to reaffirm the Church's constant teaching that contraception is a grave moral evil in the face of emerging questions concerning new fertility management technologies and dire socioeconomic predictions of overpopulation. Adding to this negative pressure was a popular optimism that promising ecumenical breakthroughs would result from changing the Church's traditional teaching. The goal of the *Theology of the Body* is to reaffirm *Humanae Vitae's* teaching and deepen its theological explanation by developing its rich scripturally revealed personalist anthropological foundations.

Humanae Vitae framed the question as a moral problematic requiring a moral analysis. The *Theology of the Body* framed the question as an anthropological problematic requiring analysis of the human person as revealed in scripture.

Humanae Vitae's methodology is primarily a deontological, objective and deductive moral analysis. It invokes the authorities of natural law, divine law, revelation and sacred tradition understood as the constant teaching of the magisterium. The *Theology of the Body's* methodology is primarily a personalist phenomenological exegesis focused on the subjective, experiential and interior dimensions of the human person as revealed in scripture. It invokes the authority of key scriptural passages and it appeals to human experience. It develops its anthropology in the hermeneutical dimensions of gift and personalism.

Humanae Vitae and the *Theology of the Body* both understand the conjugal act as the sexual uniting of husband and wife. Nevertheless, characterization of the conjugal act is different in the two teachings. *Humanae Vitae* characterizes the conjugal act in categories that facilitate *Humanae Vitae's* deontological moral analysis. Hence, the conjugal act is spoken of in terms of ends or purposes, natural law and divine law. The *Theology of the Body* characterizes the conjugal act in categories of type

93

and prototype, sign and sacrament, and ultimately as the *imago Dei*; - the image, icon, sign, or sacrament of the Blessed Trinity.

Humanae Vitae and the *Theology of the Body* focus on the conjugal act in different dimensions. *Humanae Vitae* focuses on its tropological or moral dimension. The *Theology of the Body* focuses on its anagogic dimension, which means its ultimate spiritual or mystical meaning. Nevertheless, the *Theology of the Body* and *Humanae Vitae* are in every respect mutually affirming and doctrinally consistent. *Humanae Vitae* relies primarily on an ontology or metaphysics of being and the *Theology of the Body* relies primarily on an ontology or metaphysics of person. They are grounded in different anthropologies and employ different methodologies. Nevertheless, the conjugal act remains the central focus of both treatises, which establishes their theologically homogeneous and organic continuity and bodes well for their doctrinal integration and assimilation. They each develop the theology of the conjugal act, to use Bonaventure's vocabulary, according to different "mystical senses and intelligences." *Humanae Vitae* teaches the moral sense and intelligence. The *Theology of the Body* teaches the anagogic sense and intelligence. Nevertheless, considered as two teachings, *Humanae Vitae* and the *Theology of the Body* converge at the conjugal act, and the latter can rightly be considered as an authentic development of the former, irrespective of their different ontology, anthropology, methodology, exegetical senses and intelligences, goals, framing or authorities.

✝

PART III

The *Theology of the Body* Develops *Humanae Vitae*

Introduction to Part III

Our thesis is that Pope Saint John Paul II's understanding of the conjugal act in the *Theology of the Body* develops the doctrine of *Humanae Vitae* and opens a new horizon for theological anthropology and the theology of marriage.

Part I Introduced theological anthropology, natural law theory, Personalism, ontology and the authority of papal pronouncements. Part I.1 provided examples of speculative theological anthropologies from different Church Fathers, Doctors and saints up to the scholastic period. Part I.2 summarized a contemporary articulation and application of natural law theory promulgated by the International Theological Commission with commentaries by noted theologians. Part I.3 presented Personalism as a philosophical movement and traced its origins to theology in Christianity's first centuries in which Church councils deliberated Christological controversies and defined the dogmas of the Blessed Trinity and the Hypostatic union. Part I.4 contrasted the ontology of being and the ontology of person. Part I.5 introduced the relative authority of *Humanae Vitae* and the *Theology of the Body* as papal pronouncements.

Part II compared *Humanae Vitae* and the *Theology of the Body*. It presented the relationship between the two teachings, their stated goals, the questions they sought to answer, their ways of framing the questions, their theological methodologies, authorities they invoked, and the characterizations of the conjugal act used in their respective arguments.

Part III considers the theological relationship between *Humanae Vitae*, and the *Theology of the Body*, from the point of view of doctrine and doctrinal development. Part III.1 recognizes *Humanae Vitae's* moral prohibition as settled doctrine and it establishes the conjugal act as the common subject matter and single theological root of *Humanae Vitae* and the *Theology of the Body*. Part III.2 discusses doctrinal development in general and characterizes the *Theology of the Body* as an initiative to defeat an attack on the mystery of the body represented by the widespread rejection of *Humanae Vitae*. It shows how the *Theology of the Body* develops *Humanae Vitae's* understanding of the conjugal act and responds to the attack on the mystery of the body by unfolding its mystical, anagogic and sacramental dimensions. Part III.3 presents and discusses theological and philosophical strategies and techniques John Paul used to develop the *Theology of the Body's* catechesis. It discusses how these techniques and strategies brought the *Theology of the Body's* vision into view. It recapitulates what is new in the *Theology of the Body* and what is being considered a development of doctrine. Lastly, Part III.4 characterizes the *Theology of the Body's* development of the doctrine of *Humanae Vitae* as a Nuptial and/or Spousal Mystery and shows how the theological development of this mystery may ultimately be recognized as a doctrinal development of moment, deepening our understanding of all Christian mysteries.

III.1 Relationship between *Humanae Vitae* and the *Theology of the Body* as Doctrine

III.1.1 Settled Doctrine

Humanae Vitae's prohibition of contraception is settled doctrine. A problem of our day is the pastoral failure and widespread rejection of *Humanae Vitae*. In the aftermath of *Humanae Vitae,* Catholic married couples use contraception at high rates indistinguishable from the broader population. This pastoral failure scatters the Christian fold and deconstructs Western culture. Theologians cannot avoid this problem.

According to Henri de Lubac, a longtime friend and correspondent of John Paul II, theologians must deal with the problems of their own day:

> And it follows that we cannot run away whenever we feel like it into another age…We cannot avoid the problems of our own day, any more than we can excuse ourselves from its tasks or run away from its battles. If we are to live in the Church, then we have to become involved in the problems she faces now, and the assent of our intelligence is owed to her doctrine as we find it set out today.[148]

III.1.2 Common Subject Matter

The conjugal act is the subject matter of *Humanae Vitae* and *Humanae Vitae* is the subject matter of the *Theology of the Body*. We are instructed by the *Theology of the Body* that the part of its catechesis devoted to *Humanae Vitae* is united to all the other parts of the *Theology of the Body* organically and homogeneously: "because *it is from this topic* [*Humanae Vitae*] *that the questions spring* that run in some way through the whole

---

[148] Henri Cardinal de Lubac, S.J., *The Splendor of the Church*, trans. Michael Mason (New York: Sheed and Ward, 1956), 6.

of our reflections." (TOB 133.4) And: "In some sense, one can even say that all the reflections dealing with the 'Redemption of the Body and the Sacramentality of Marriage' *seem* to constitute *an extensive commentary* on the doctrine contained precisely in *Humanae Vitae*." (TOB 133.2)

It is, therefore, the moral doctrine of *Humanae Vitae* that the *Theology of the Body* proposes to develop, which is formulated "…each and every marriage act must remain open to the transmission of life (HV 8)." The *Theology of the Body* proposes "to deepen the explanation of Christian truth in this area." (TOB 133.2,5) Specifically, it proposes a deeper theological explanation of the unitive and procreative meanings *Humanae Vitas* invokes:

> That teaching, often set forth by the magisterium, is founded upon the inseparable connection, willed by God and unable to be broken by man on his own initiative, between the two meanings of the conjugal act: the unitive meaning and the procreative meaning. (HV 12)

The deepening proposed by the *Theology of the Body* explicates the anagogic dimensions of the conjugal act; that is, its ultimate spiritual and mystical meanings in a manner that is organically and homogeneously continuous with *Humanae Vitae*. Organic and homogeneous continuity is only possible because the conjugal act is the common subject matter of both teachings.

As the *Theology of the Body* deepens and strengthens the theological understanding of the unitive and procreative meanings of the conjugal act, it simultaneously deepens and strengthens *Humanae Vitae's* anthropological foundation and broadens its theological signification.

III.1.3 Doctrinal Development

Recognizing that the *Theology of the Body* is an extended commentary on the doctrine of *Humanae Vitae* only raises the question but does not establish that the *Theology of the Body* is a genuine development of *Humanae Vitae's* doctrine. Genuine developments of doctrine are usually recognized as such only in hindsight after early formulations are refined, and finally declared and promulgated by the magisterium. Rival formulations of budding developments may simmer in the mind of the faithful, the *sensus fidelium*, for centuries. With the passage of time and convergences of historical circumstances, frequently precipitated by crises, the simmering development boils over. Our interest is in whether the *Theology of the Body,* which is currently simmering in an atmosphere of crisis, will ultimately be refined, declared authoritatively and promulgated as a genuine doctrinal development at some time in the future. That sort of future unfolding is famously prognosticated as likely in George Weigel's biography of John Paul, where he describes the *Theology of the Body* as a theological time bomb. "The Church and the world will be well into the twenty-first century, and perhaps far beyond, before Catholic Theology has fully assimilated these 130 general audience addresses."[149]

Today, the Church and theologians struggle with effects of demystification of the body. Paraphrasing de Lubac, we cannot excuse ourselves from this task, nor run away from this battle, nor avoid this challenge. The body is an endowment of our Creator. The mystery of the body is essential to all Christian Mysteries and the entire patrimony of the Church. Therefore, our theology must take the measure of the body, of its mystery, and discern its relevance anew. Applying de Lubac's understanding of the theologian's responsibility to respond to attacks on the foundations of the faith, we can say with de Lubac that if the body is

---

[149] George Weigel, *Witness to Hope* (Baltimore: Cliff Street Books, 2001), 342.

demystified "...the whole inheritance of Tradition, hitherto held without question, becomes, in one way or another, disputed territory."[150]

De Lubac describes, how theology responds when an essential foundation of its Sacred Tradition, like the body, is subjected to this sort of mammoth assault:

> The thing seems to have become a burden rather than a source of vitality, and thus to constitute an obstruction to the very life which it is supposed to feed and transmit. And that is the situation in which it becomes imperative to reflect upon what one previously lived unthinkingly. The full bloodedness of primitive naïveté becomes a thing of the past, and one has to stand back and "objectify." When something is called into question you have to get down to its roots. If you are to meet the strategic demands of the situation, and if you are to be rational in retaining what others reject, the whole matter has to be studied from a new viewpoint. It is not so much a question of justifying as elucidating; polemic is not the primary concern. Fundamentally, what you feel is a need to see straight; it is a time for stocktaking.[151]

De Lubac captures exactly the spirit in which John Paul read the signs of the times, recognized the rejection of *Humanae Vitae* as an attack on the foundations of theology and responded with the *Theology of the Body*.

III.2 An Attack on the Foundations of Theology

The *Theology of the Body* presents a new viewpoint from which to meet the strategic demands of the situation created by demystification of the body.

---

[150] de Lubac, 4.
[151] Ibid.

The new viewpoint is a nuptial or spousal understanding of the body or the Nuptial / Spousal Mystery.

We saw that John Paul explicitly connects the *Theology of the Body* to *Humanae Vitae* only at the end of the *Theology of the Body*, where, in the final reflection he says: "...that part... located at the end is at the same time found at the beginning..." (TOB 133.4) He explains, in other words, that the part of the catechesis devoted to *Humanae Vitae*, with which the entire *Theology of the Body* catechesis is organically and homogeneously related, is not only its finale, but also its starting point. The doctrine of *Humanae Vitae* is the root and branch, the alpha and omega, of John Paul's *Theology of the Body*.

Genuine developments integrate with other doctrines by assimilation thereby deepening and enriching our understanding of all doctrines. An outline of John Paul's proposal shows that the *Theology of the Body* does affect many other mysteries and doctrines. Thus, it potentially deepens and enriches the way we understand other Christian mysteries. What, then, is the vision of the *Theology of the Body*?

III.2.1 The *Theology of the Body's* Vision -In Brief

The moral doctrine of *Humanae Vitae* being developed is formulated: "...each and every marriage act must remain open to the transmission of life." (HV 11) The *Theology of the Body* is a proposal "to deepen the explanation of Christian truth in this area." (TOB 133.2,5) The specific development proposed is a deeper theological explanation of *Humanae Vitae's* references to the unitive and procreative meanings of the conjugal act. The proposed theological development explicates the ultimate spiritual and mystical meaning of the conjugal act; that is, its anagogic dimensions. The *Theology of the Body* offers a deeper, loftier and broader understanding of the unitive and procreative meanings of the conjugal act in organic and homogeneous continuity with *Humanae Vitae*. In this way the *Theology of the Body* strengthens *Humanae Vitae's* moral teaching, deepens *Humanae Vitae's* anthropological foundation, clarifies *Humanae Vitae's* call to exalted holiness and greatly broadens *Humanae Vitae's* theological horizon.

The *Theology of the Body* is rich in mystical themes which include the mysteries of creation, redemption, sacraments, vocations, and sanctification in the here and now and in eternal life. It unites all these themes and others to its overarching theme of the mystical and sacramental dimensions of marriage, the one flesh union of man and woman, the conjugal act.

The *Theology of the Body* opens its exposition of the truth of Christian marriage immediately in the first of its presentations. Jesus and Pharisees discuss divorce (Mt 19:3-8), and Jesus steers the conversation to the overall structure of things in the beginning. Jesus interprets Genesis 2:24: "For this reason a man shall leave his father and mother and unite with his wife, and the two will be one flesh." Jesus teaches the Pharisees that marriage was created to be indissoluble: "the two shall become one. So, they are no longer two but one. What therefore God has joined together, let no man put asunder." (Mt. 19:5-6).

With indissolubility established, John Paul scrutinizes other details in the Genesis accounts of the mystery of Creation to develop a theology of marriage that holds the entire catechesis together. The line of development connects Christ's teaching on the indissolubility of marriage: to the development of a theology of marriage in the mystery of Creation; to development of marriage as a primordial sacrament and as a Sacrament of the Church; to the development of marriage as prophetic of our eschatological participation in Trinitarian life; to development of renunciation of marriage and the embrace of consecrated virginity to witness to the truth of the kingdom of heaven; and finally, to John Paul's disclosure of the connection between the *Theology of the Body* to the doctrinal tradition.

Moving on from the dialogue with the Pharisees, the *Theology of the Body's* analyses derive these precepts: that God's plan to make man "in our image after our likeness" (Gn. 1:26) refers to man, plural, male and female (TOB 5.3); that their one flesh union (TOB 10.2), as a communion of persons, in the moment of communion, images the inscrutable divine Communion of Persons, the Blessed Trinity (TOB 9.3); that this structure of communion of man and woman in indissoluble mutual self-gift is the foundation of ethics and culture (TOB 45.3); that it constitutes an inalienable norm for a theological understanding of man (TOB 9.5); and that it is perhaps the deepest theological aspect of everything that can be said about man (TOB 9.3).

These precepts propose a theological understanding of marriage; the one flesh union of man and woman, the conjugal act. The terms one flesh union, conjugal act, and marriage act are interchangeable. John Paul II explicitly states that the one flesh union of man and woman is expressed and realized in the conjugal act (TOB 10.2).

The *Theology of the Body* further develops the theology of the sacramentality of marriage to include: that marriage is a primordial sacrament from pre-history in the mystery of Creation 19.4); that as a primordial sacrament it is the foundation of the whole sacramental order because it images the Blessed Trinity, and it foreshadows the Paschal mystery and the new economy of salvation (TOB 98.2); and in addition, that the primordial sacrament of marriage is transposed into history as the sacrament of Christ's redemptive love for the Church (TOB 95.7).

Going still further in considering marriage as a sacrament, the *Theology of the Body* develops Saint Paul's theology of marriage by tracing marriage back from its existence as a Christian sacrament to its existence as a primordial sacrament and further back to its existence as "the plan of the mystery hidden from ages past in God." (Eph. 3:9). (TOB 94.2) In other words, the *Theology of the Body* develops Paul's teaching on the great mystery, the *mysterium magnum* of Ephesians (Eph. 5:32), to be understood to mean that marriage in its mystical dimension encompasses the entire sacramental order and order of grace. (TOB 95b.4)

The foregoing outlines John Paul's development of the anagogic, mystical, spiritual and sacramental dimensions of the conjugal act. These statements point out the *Theology of the Body's* great enlargement of the theological scope of the meaning of the unitive and procreative dimensions of the conjugal act, and the breadth and depth of its implications. These statements also attest to the *Theology of the Body's* inherent, and resolutely fearless, call for assimilation of its teaching with the whole body of Christian doctrine.

Having developed and connected the indissolubility of marriage, the theological meaning of the conjugal act, the primordial sacramentality of marriage, the historical sacramentality of Holy Matrimony as the sacrament of the Church, the *magnum mysterium* of *Eph. 5: 32*, and the *mystery hidden from eternity in God* of *Eph. 3: 9*, the *Theology of the Body* discloses, in its final reflection, its connection to Church doctrine, as cited previously:

> In some sense, one can even say that all the reflections dealing with the "Redemption of the Body and the Sacramentality of Marriage" *seem* to constitute *an extensive commentary* on the doctrine contained precisely in *Humanae Vitae*." (TOB 133.2)

John Paul reinforced this connection between the encyclical *Humanae Vitae* and his *Theology of the Body*, attested to their mutually harmonious relationship and integrated both pastoral initiatives for our present age, in the excerpt, also cited previously:

> ...*it is from this topic that the questions spring* that run in some way through the whole of our reflections. It follows that this final part [The catecheses devoted to *Humanae Vitae*] is not artificially added to the whole [*Theology of the Body*], but is organically and homogeneously united with it. (TOB 133.4)

The *Theology of the Body* is a mystically rich theological proposal that develops the doctrine of *Humanae Vitae* in height, breadth and depth, and unflinchingly calls for integration and assimilation with established doctrine in all of its dimensions.

In terms of depth, the *Theology of the Body* develops the moral doctrine of *Humanae Vitae* by identifying the conjugal act exegetically and theologically as a mystical image of the Blessed Trinity, in addition to being the *mysterium magnum* of the relationship between Christ and the Church of *Eph. 5: 32*, and the *mystery hidden from eternity in God of Eph. 3:9*. This inference of imaging of the Blessed Trinity, as a scriptural interpretation, goes beyond the boundaries of analogy. Analogy always presupposes dissimilarity as it allows similarity. The mystical sense of image exceeds this limitation of analogy, simile, metaphor and the like. Instead, as used theologically, image belongs to a mystical category which includes image, icon, sign and sacrament. This mystical category describes types that not only evoke their prototype but also connote a mystical participation between the type and the prototype of which it is an image, icon, sign or sacrament. Similarly, the mystical sense of sign is understood theologically as a natural type that points to and mystically participates in a supernatural prototype. The sense of sacrament, moreover, is understood to effect what it signifies.

By transcending the constraints of analogy, metaphor and simile, this scripturally grounded mystical symbolism unfolds the anagogic dimensions of the conjugal act, -its ultimate mystical and spiritual meaning. The language of icon, image, sign and sacrament, unmasks and makes manifest the hidden holiness in the total, sincere and irrevocable mutual self-giving of the conjugal act (TOB 19.5).

The anagogic meaning becomes intelligible by reading the language of the body in truth. The final catecheses which take up *Humanae Vitae* juxtapose reading the language of the body in truth, as a horizon of holiness, alongside contraception, its counterfeit, which holds back, withdraws outwardly and inwardly and in self-withholding, misreads the truth of the language of the body. (See TOB 124.6-7)

It is difficult to exaggerate the magnificence of the *Theology of the Body's* vision of conjugal love. George Weigel expressed it as follows:

105

The Theology of Marriage and Celibacy ends with John Paul's most dramatic celebration of marital love. Sexual love, he concludes, is an act of worship. "Conjugal life becomes…liturgical" when the "language of the body" becomes the means to encounter, through an experience of the sacred, what God had willed for the world and for humanity "from the beginning." The sexual gift of self, freely offered and freely received within the covenant of marriage, becomes a way to sanctify the world.[152]

…it may prove to be the decisive moment in exorcising the Manichaean demon and its deprecation of human sexuality from Catholic moral theology."[153]

III.3 How does the *Theology of the Body* develop its catechesis to bring its vision into view?

Anthropology is foundational to ethics or moral doctrine. Moral doctrine concerns what is good and not good for man and anthropology supplies the baseline understanding of man that gives meaning to the moral doctrine. The *Theology of the Body* proposes an enlargement of *Humanae Vitae's* theological anthropology and, hence, an enlargement of its theological foundation for ethics or moral theology.

The anthropology proposed by the *Theology of the Body* deepens but does not discard or destroy the anthropology of *Humanae Vitae*. *Humanae Vitae's* theological anthropology is mediated primarily by a naturalistic philosophical anthropology. The *Theology of the Body's* theological anthropology is mediated primarily by a personalistic philosophical anthropology. The *Theology of the Body* uses personalist anthropology as a scriptural hermeneutic to deepen our understanding of the revealed

---

[152] Weigel, 341.
[153] Ibid., 342.

origin and foundation of the conjugal act. In doing so, it develops our understanding of the sacramental summits the conjugal act signifies.

The dominant anthropology undergirding *Humanae Vitae* is the Boethian definition of the human person as a rational animal.[154] However, it would be wrong to think that the entire Catholic tradition of natural law is spoken for by this contribution of Boethius. The Catholic natural law tradition is richer than a simplistic adoption of Boethian anthropology. It is enriched by the scripturally warranted understanding that the divine law is written in human hearts (Rom. 2:15). Thus, as *Humanae Vitae* noted, divine revelation illuminates and enriches the natural moral law.

> Such questions required from the teaching authority of the Church a new and deeper reflection upon the principles of moral teaching on marriage: a teaching founded on the natural law, illuminated and enriched by divine revelation. (HV 4)

Nevertheless, the polemics that followed the promulgation of *Humanae Vitae* predominantly construed natural law in naturalistic terms at the expense of the illuminating influences of scripture and tradition. The *Theology of the Body*, by contrast and in line with de Lubac's counsel, bracketed or put aside these polemics and sought instead to discern anew what scripture itself actually discloses concerning the conjugal act without naturalistic mediation. In this way the *Theology of the Body* develops a mystical understanding of the conjugal embrace: as an image of the Blessed Trinity; as a sacramental sign of God's love for his people; a sign of the covenant between God and Israel; and of the New Covenant between Christ and the Church. As a communion of persons open to the blessing of fertility, the conjugal embrace is developed as a type of its Prototype, the Blessed Trinity. As the *Magnum Mysterium* of Ephesians 5:31, the conjugal embrace signifies Christ's love for the Church and the

---

[154] See: Personalism and Natural Law, (Part I.3b above)

mystery hidden in God from eternity of Ephesians 3:9. As an efficacious sign of the New Covenant, the conjugal embrace is a sacramental sign of the Paschal Mystery and the Eucharist. Moreover, the *Theology of the Body* develops the conjugal embrace as an image and sacramental sign of eschatological divinization. By these significations the *Theology of the Body* develops the ultimate spiritual and mystical, or anagogic, dimensions of the conjugal embrace.

Said another way, John Paul II's *Theology of the Body* brought a vision of the Christian mysteries of Creation, Redemption and Sanctification, vocations, grace and sacraments into view all unified in a sacramental presentation of Christian Marriage.

John Paul brought this comprehensive catechesis and theological vision of marriage into view by applying a mix of relatively modern techniques and strategies to the interpretation of key scriptural passages. The first technique he employed was to bracket the ontology or metaphysics of being, its philosophical anthropology and its deontological mediation of natural law reasoning described above in Part I.2. This methodology follows Boethian rational animal anthropology and a teleological premise that discrete beings achieve perfection and fulfill their purpose by acting according to their natures. This methodology produces objective, realist arguments and deduces categorical ethical norms from the nature and purpose of existing things.

John Paul, however, did not think this approach was well suited to the discovery of the ultimate mystical and spiritual meanings of the conjugal act and used a different strategy to reach these dimensions. Through a technique of bracketing, the *Theology of the Body* suspends naturalistic deontological reduction in favor of analyses that are personalistic rather than naturalistic, subjective rather than objective, experiential rather than categorical, a posteriori rather than a priori, and inductive rather than deductive.

John Paul expressed the difference between objective reductive, and subjective inductive analysis in an article written in 1975 entitled

Subjectivity and the Irreducible in the Human Being, which was quoted (See Part I.3.c; p.45) and is repeated here following an introductory paragraph:

In order to interpret the human being in the context of lived experience, the aspect of *consciousness* must be introduced into the analysis of human existence. The human being is then given to us not merely as a being defined according to species, but as a concrete self, a self-experiencing subject. Our own subjective being and the existence proper to it (that of a *suppositum*) appear to us in experience precisely as a self-experiencing subject. If we pause here, this being discloses the structures that determine it as a concrete self. The disclosure of these structures constituting the human self-need in no way signify a break with reduction and the species definition of a human being– rather, it signifies the kind of methodological operation that may be described as *pausing at the irreducible*. We should pause in the process of reduction, which leads us in the direction of understanding the human being in the world (a *cosmological* type of understanding), in order to understand the human being inwardly. This later type of understanding may be called *personalistic*. The personalistic type of understanding the human being is not the antinomy of the cosmological type but its complement. As I mentioned earlier, the definition of the person formulated by Boethius only marks out the "metaphysical terrain" for interpreting the personal subjectivity of the human being.

The experience of the human being cannot be derived by way of cosmological reduction; we must pause at the irreducible at that which is unique and unrepeatable in each human being, by virtue of which he or she is not just *a particular human being* –an individual of a certain species– but *a personal subject*. Only then do we get a true and complete picture of the human being. We cannot complete this picture through reduction alone; we also cannot remain within the framework of the irreducible alone (for then we would be unable to get beyond the pure self). The one must be cognitively supplemented with the other. Nevertheless, given the variety of circumstances of the real existence of human beings, we must always leave the greater space in this cognitive effort for the irreducible; we must, as it were, give the irreducible the upper hand about the human being, both in theory and practice. For the irreducible also refers to everything in the human being that is invisible and wholly internal and whereby each human being, myself included, is an "eyewitness" of his or her own self –of his or her own humanity and person. [155]

Personalism (see Part I.3), seeks to understand the subjectivity, interiority and experience of persons. Ontologically, personalism gives priority to the singular unrepeatable and incommunicable personal subject, which is very different from naturalism and an ontology of being which classifies objects categorically.

A cardinal principle of personalism is that to be a person is to be in relation with other persons. There is no such thing as a person without being in relation with other persons. Recall, as explained in Part 13, our common contemporary understanding of the meaning of the term person entered human language from the early Ecumenical Councils that defined the Blessed Trinity as one God in three *Persons*, and the hypostatic union in Christ as one *Person* having two natures, one human and one divine. Prior to these dogmatic definitions the term person merely designated

---

[155] Wojtyla, 213-4.

a function or role. After these dogmatic definitions the term person acquired its present day meaning and over time incommunicability and personal freedom displaced social or cosmological determinism as the hallmark of persons.

The idea that freedom is the hallmark of persons, rather than social or cosmological determinism, implies that persons have the capacity to give themselves as gifts. This capacity of persons is essential to the *Theology of the Body's* understanding of the sacramentality of marriage:

> Man *is a person precisely because he is master of himself and has dominion over himself.* Indeed, inasmuch as he is master over himself, he can "give himself" to another. And it is this dimension—the dimension of the freedom of the gift—that becomes essential and decisive for the "language of the body" in which man and woman express themselves reciprocally in conjugal union. (TOB 123.5)

Lastly, John Paul's methodology is descriptive or phenomenological and inductive. It explores its subject matter in great detail from many perspectives in order to construct, inductively, an accurate composite picture of what the subject discloses.

These are techniques and strategies the *Theology of the Body* applies to the interpretation of key passages in scripture to develop a theology of marriage to such a degree that marriage itself becomes a hermeneutic for understanding the mysteries of the Blessed Trinity, the Hypostatic Union, the Paschal Mystery, the Eucharist and eschatological divinization. A new theological pathway for understanding all these mysteries is opened by a new understanding of the mystical and spiritual dimensions of marriage explicated in the *Theology of the Body*.

An argument is sometimes made that the *Theology of the Body* offers nothing new that doesn't appear in some form in the theological anthropologies like those we reviewed in Part I Chapter 1. This argument would hold that the Church has always recognized the goodness of marriage.

There is some truth and some untruth to this objection. Yes, the Church always recognized the goodness of marriage. However, her theology of marriage actually developed very slowly over two millennia and continues being debated today. Accordingly, it is reasonable to regard marriage as an area ripe for theological development. The theological vision of marriage in John Paul's *Theology of the Body* may be decisive in resolving contemporary anomalous understandings of marriage that gained popularity in the wake of *Humanae Vitae's* pastoral failure. The *Theology of the Body* may prevail even if contemporary theological establishments underestimate, mute or misconstrue its contribution. Some ignore the *Theology of the Body* because it is not easy to apprehend. Others have prior commitments to which it is uncongenial. Nevertheless, it would seem that Pope Saint John Paul is as bold and unflinching in his *Theology of the Body*, or maybe even more so, than he was in facing down Soviet Communism.

The last part of this dissertation considers doctrinal development in detail. Here, however, it may be well to recapitulate exactly what is new and what precisely will be considered as a development of doctrine.

The conjugal act is the subject of the encyclical *Humanae Vitae*. John Paul instructs us that the *Theology of the Body* is a commentary on the doctrine of *Humanae Vitae*. Hence, the *Theology of the Body* is an extended commentary on the theological meaning of conjugal acts.

The conjugal act is the *sine qua non* of marriage. The conjugal act in a micro sense is the act of man and wife uniting in sexual intercourse. The conjugal act in a macro sense is the act of man and wife uniting in indissoluble marriage until death. What John Paul teaches in the *Theology of the Body* is that the conjugal act, micro and macro, is a sacramental sign and image of God the Blessed Trinity and a sacramental sign and image of Christ's love for the Church manifest in all Christian mysteries including the Incarnation, Paschal and Eucharistic Mysteries:

112

Baptism draws its essential signification and sacramental strength from the Redeemer's spousal love through which above all the sacramentality of the Church herself is constituted, the *sacramentum magnum*. One can perhaps say the same thing also about the *Eucharist*, which seems to be indicated by the following words about the nourishment of one's own body: everyone nourishes and cares for his body "as Christ does with the Church, because we are members of his body" (Eph 5:29-30). In fact, Christ nourishes the church with his Body precisely in the Eucharist. (TOB 99.1)

In the *Theology of the Body* these deepest and highest of Christian mysteries are offered as the paradigm and a basis of the intelligibility of the conjugal act, micro and macro, and the conjugal act is in turn offered as a basis of the intelligibility of these highest of Christian mysteries. More, vocations in this life and divinization in eternal life or the eschaton are understood through the same spousal prism and paradigm of mutual personal self-gift between man and wife and between God and man. Accordingly, the *Theology of the Body* develops *Humanae Vitae's* unitive and procreative doctrine and establishes the conjugal act as a ground of intelligibility for the Blessed Trinity, the *mysterium magnum* of Ephesians 5:31, and the mystery hidden in God from eternity of Ephesians 3:9.

III.4 The Conjugal Act: Type, Image and Sign of the Blessed Trinity

The *Theology of the Body* proposes to deepen *Humanae Vitae's* theological explanation of its doctrine that conjugal acts must be open to the transmission of life. According to *Humanae Vitae*:

This particular doctrine, often expounded by the magisterium of the Church, is based on the inseparable connection, established by God, which man on his own initiative may not break, between the unitive significance and the procreative significance which are both inherent to the marriage act. (HV 12)

The *Theology of the Body* understands the conjugal act to include indissoluble marriage. Both are mutually inclusive and inextricable:

> Marriage as a sacrament is contracted by means of *the word*, which is *a sacramental sign in virtue of its content*, "I take you as my wife/as my husband, and I promise to be faithful to you always, in joy and in sorrow, in sickness and in health, and to love and honor you all the days of my life." However, this sacramental word is, of itself, only a sign of the coming to be of marriage. And the coming to be of marriage is distinct from its consummation, so much so that without this consummation, marriage is not yet constituted in its full reality. (TOB 103.2)

The *Theology of the Body* explains the sacramental, mystical, spiritual and anagogic dimensions of conjugal acts in order to deepen *Humanae Vitae's* theological explanation of its doctrine by proposing that the 'communion of persons' man and woman form 'from the beginning' is an image, sign and type of the Blessed Trinity:

> ...we can deduce that *man became the" image of God" not only through his humanity but also through the communion of persons* which man and woman form from the very beginning. The function of the image is that of mirroring the one who is the model, of reproducing its own prototype. Man becomes an image of God not

so much in the moment of solitude as in the moment of communion. He is, in fact, "from the beginning" not only an image in which the solitude of one Person, who rules the world, mirrors itself, but also and essentially the image of an inscrutable divine communion of Persons. (TOB 9.3)

This chapter discusses the range of sacramental signification of the conjugal act. It shows how, according to the *Theology of the Body*, conjugal acts sacramentally signify: the imminent Blessed Trinity as its type and image; and the economic Blessed Trinity in activities of Creation, Redemption and Sanctification. It shows how, according to the *Theology of the Body*, the conjugal act is paradigmatic of grace and the foundation of the sacramental order.

III.4.1 Conjugal Acts Signify the Imminent Blessed Trinity

The *Theology of the Body* unfolds the mystical dimensions of conjugal acts in the context of the above-mentioned co-inherence and inextricability of indissoluble marriage and the one flesh union of man and wife. Indissolubility is essential to conjugal acts and is the apt context by which to signify the eternal attribute of the Blessed Trinity. A dissoluble union could not signify the eternal Blessed Trinity.

The *Theology of the Body* interprets the two Genesis narratives that describe the creation of man in a manner that authorizes us to understand that conjugal acts signify the immanent Blessed Trinity. The *Theology of the Body* explains that using plural personal pronouns "us" and "our," in the text, "let us make man in our image, in our likeness" (Gen 1:27), communicates plurality in God. The *Theology of the Body* explains, further, that the noun 'man' is also to be understood as plural and includes both male and female. It explains that the plurality of man in this text images the plurality in God.

Also, the charge to "Be fruitful and multiply, fill the earth, subdue it, and rule" (Gen. 1:28) conveys fruitfulness to man, an image of God's fruitfulness. The charge to "rule" communicates dominion, imaging God's dominion, and the charge to "rule" also communicates freedom, imaging God's freedom, inasmuch as dominion and rule cannot be deterministic and therefore imply freedom.

The Genesis narratives which intimate God's eternity, plurality, freedom, fruitfulness and dominion, call for a theology of God as eternal, plural, free, fruitful and lordly, or having dominion. Likewise, intimations of man's plurality, freedom, fruitfulness and dominion intimate a theology of man in which sexual differentiation, freedom, fruitfulness and dominion constitute God's image and signify the immanent Blessed Trinity.

The *Theology of the Body* understands further development of man's plurality, freedom, fruitfulness and dominion to be intimated by Genesis 2:24: "For this reason a man shall leave his father and mother and unite with his wife, and the two will be one flesh." (Gen. 2:24) Here, man's plurality, freedom, fruitfulness and dominion are directly and specifically connected with conjugal acts. Unity in plurality is intimated by one flesh union. According to the *Theology of the Body*: "The unity about which Genesis 2:24 speaks, ("and the two will be one flesh"), is without doubt the unity that is expressed and realized in the conjugal act." (TOB 10.2). According to the *Theology of the Body*, the unity in plurality of the one flesh union of man and wife authorizes us to take the further step of understanding conjugal acts to signify the Blessed Trinity:

> Since they are formed in the image of God also inasmuch as they form an authentic communion of persons, the first man and the first woman must constitute the beginning and model of that communion for all men and women who in any period unite with each other so intimately that they are "one flesh." (TOB 10.3)

The concepts of 'person' and 'communion' are central in the philosophical and theological work of John Paul. So much so that *Person and Communion* is the title of a book of his selected essays. These writings detail different meanings supported by different ways of speaking about human persons individually and in communal association. For our purpose, which is to grasp the depth of meaning of communion of persons, it is sufficient to recall that the meaning of the term person was transformed into its present meaning by the Council of Nicaea in 325 AD. The council fathers adopted the term person for the dogmatic definition of the Blessed Trinity as one God in three divine persons. The term person was used again by the council of Chalcedon in 451AD to dogmatically define the hypostatic union of divine and human natures, -unconfused, immutable, indivisible and inseparable- in the person of Jesus Christ (Chapter 3).

The signification of plurality, freedom, fruitfulness and dominion is strengthened by the communion of persons formed by one flesh union of Adam and Eve which signifies the divine Communion of Persons, the Blessed Trinity. The *Theology of the Body* explains this signification as follows:

> The account of the creation of man in Genesis 1 affirms from the beginning and directly that man was created in the image of God inasmuch as he is male and female. The account of Genesis 2, by contrast, does not speak of the "image of God," but reveals, in the manner proper to it, that the complete and definitive creation of "man" ...expresses itself in giving life to the "*communio personarum*" that man and woman form. (TOB 9.3)

Further on in the same passage John Paul concludes that:

> ...we can deduce that man became the image of God not only through his own humanity, but also through the

communion of persons, which man and woman form from the very beginning. (TOB 9.3)

And reinforcing the conclusion, he continues:

He is, in fact, 'from the beginning' not only an image in which the solitude of one Person who rules the world, mirrors itself, but also and essentially the image of an inscrutable divine Communion of Persons. (TOB 9.3).

So far, we have indicated how the *Theology of the Body* proposes that conjugal acts, understood in their indissolubility, unity in plurality, fruitfulness, freedom, dominion and communion of persons, signify the immanent Blessed Trinity. We also considered that this exegesis of the Genesis creation stories owes its intelligibility to the creation and use of the term 'person,' that traces its contemporary meaning to the dogmatic definitions of the Blessed Trinity (Nicaea) and the hypostatic union in Jesus Christ (Chalcedon).

III.4.2 Conjugal Acts Signify the Economic Blessed Trinity

The *Theology of the Body* teaches that conjugal acts signify the immanent Blessed Trinity according to scripture and tradition. Next we consider how the *Theology of the Body* teaches that conjugal acts signify the activity of the economic Blessed Trinity in Creation, Redemption and Sanctification.

III.4.2a The Conjugal Act and the Mystery of Creation

How does the *Theology of the Body* teach that conjugal acts signify the mystery of Creation? According to the *Theology of the Body* man shares in the ongoing mystery of Creation. He is a co-creator with God in the mystery of Creation which unfolds continuously until the consummation of the world. Each time man and wife unite in conjugal acts, they recall the original mystery of the Creation of man: they participate as co-creators in the continuing mystery of Creation; and they anticipate, foreshadow or prophesize the consummation of the mystery of Creation in the world to come:

> When both unite so intimately with each other that they become 'one flesh,'...each union of this kind renews in some way the mystery of creation in all its original depth and vital power. "Taken from the man" as "flesh from his flesh," the woman consequently becomes, as "wife" and through her motherhood, mother of the living (Gen. 3:20), because her motherhood has its proper origin also in him. Procreation is rooted in creation, and every time it reproduces in some way its mystery. (TOB 10.4)

Hence, as conjugal acts recall and participate in the mystery of Creation, they likewise foreshadow the consummation of Creation when Christ will unite the Church, notably, -as His body and his bride-, to Himself.

In this way, right from the beginning, conjugal acts image the economic Blessed Trinity by recalling, participating in and foreshadowing the Mystery of Creation.

III.4.2b The Conjugal Act and the Mystery of Redemption

How does the *Theology of the Body* teach that conjugal acts signify the mystery of Redemption?

Historically, the mystery of Redemption includes the birth, death and resurrection of Jesus Christ. Theologically, the mystery of Redemption includes all of history, pre-history and post-history, and is the reason for history; history's *raison d'être*. According to the *Theology of the Body*, the mystery of Redemption is the whole perspective of the Gospel: "This [i.e. redemption] is, in fact, the perspective of the whole Gospel, of the whole teaching, even more, of the whole mission of Christ." (TOB 49.3) And elsewhere: "Everything we have tried to do in the course of our meditations in order to understand the words of Christ has its definitive foundation in the mystery of the redemption of the body." (TOB 86.8) And, to repeat: "In some sense one can even say that all the reflections dealing with the 'Redemption of the Body and the Sacramentality of Marriage' *seem* to constitute *an extensive commentary* on the doctrine contained precisely in *Humanae Vitae*. (TOB 133.2). So, as with the mystery of Creation, the conjugal act recalls, participates in, and foreshadows the mystery of Redemption.

Moreover, the *Theology of the Body* references Old Testament resources to teach that the conjugal act recalls the mystery of Redemption. It shows that the spousal or nuptial covenant was the principal analogy Old Testament prophets used to teach the Israelites as God's chosen ones about their relationship with God. The *Theology of the Body* refers to Isaiah, Hosea, Ezekiel, and others, as well as psalms and the historical and wisdom literature, to demonstrate the persistence of the spousal analogy used to such an extent that Israel's transgressions are described in terms of adulterous infidelity. The *Theology of the Body* reinforces the point of this analogy:

> *Yet at the basis of* all *these statements* of the prophets stands the explicit *conviction* that the love of Yahweh for the Chosen People can and must be compared to the love that unites bride and bridegroom, the love that should unite spouses. (TOB 94.7)

The *Theology of the Body* cites Isaiah's prophetic poem to illustrate the unmistakable direct analogical linkage between Christ's divinely initiated redemptive act of mercy to Israel, wiping away the consequences of her infidelities, and the remediation of broken marital relationships:

Do not fear, for you will no longer blush;
do not be ashamed, for you will no longer be dishonored;
for you will forget the shame of your youth,
and the dishonor of your widowhood you will remember
no more.
For your Creator is your husband,
LORD of hosts is his name;
the Holy One of Israel is your Redeemer,
the God of the whole earth he is called.
The LORD calls you back,
For like a wife forsaken and grieved in spirit the Lord
has called you.
Is the wife of one's youth cast off, says your God?
For a brief moment I abandoned you,
but with immense love I will take you again.
In overflowing wrath for a moment, I hid my face
from you,
but with everlasting affection I have had compassion
on you,
says the LORD, your Redeemer.
This is like the days of Noah for me,
When I swore then that the waters of Noah would never
again go
over the earth,
so, I swear now that I will not to be angry with you
and will not threaten you.
For even if the mountains depart
and the hills are removed,
my steadfast affection shall not depart from you,
and my covenant of peace shall not waver,
says the LORD, who has compassion on you. (Isa.
54:4-10)
(TOB 95.1)

The *Theology of the Body* shows how Old Testament sources like this sample from Isaiah, lavishly elaborate the spousal analogy to portray spousal fidelity, adultery and remediation, as the pattern of the relationship between God and Israel.

In addition to Old Testament resources the *Theology of the Body* teaches that the spousal model is also employed in the New Testament, especially in Ephesians 5:22-33, to describe the spousal relationship between Christ and the Church.

The meanings drawn from the analogy in Ephesians builds on the Old Testament analogy and at the same time deepens it considerably. First, the *Theology of the Body* points out that in Ephesians, Paul is talking to the baptized. This is important from the standpoint that his hearers are already formed in the faith, in Redemption and in the Resurrection. Second, unlike the Old Testament analogy, Ephesians 5 is hortatory concerning marriage and directly applies the reciprocal love between Christ and the Church to teach how husbands are to love their wives and wives are to love their husbands. Thus, Christ's redemptive act, the mystery of Redemption, which is the perspective of the entire Gospel, is given to Christians as the model of the spousal covenant; and the spousal covenant is given to the faithful as the model of the mystery of Redemption. The conjugal act in its indissoluble dimension corresponds to the irrevocable gift of Christ to the Church and recalls the mystery of the Redemption.

Furthermore, the *Theology of the Body* teaches that the union of Christ's radical self-gift to the Church, as his bride and his body, is paradigmatic of the union of spouses' radical, mutual self-gift in intimate one flesh union, -the conjugal act. In these ways, conjugal acts in their macro and micro senses participate in the mystery of the Redemption.

Similarly, the conjugal act, by recollecting and participating in the Mystery of Redemption, foreshadows the completion of the Mystery of Redemption by which the Church and its members, the bride and body of Christ, are to be 'taken again' (Isa. 54:8) and fully united with him in Paradise. This complete unity of Christ and the Church, begun sacramentally in this life, is the Mystery of Sanctification by which we are divinized.

III.4.2c The Conjugal Act and the Mystery of Sanctification

How does the *Theology of the Body* teach that conjugal acts signify the mystery of Sanctification? Sanctification is the mystery of radical and total union with God, or our divinization, in the world to come. Our divinization is the goal of the mysteries of Creation and Redemption and, like them, it is initiated by God. Sanctification is the mystery of Christ's radical, total and irrevocable self-gift to the sanctified. It begins within history; it fulfills history, and in divinizing the sanctified, completes history in eternal life.

According to the *Theology of the Body*, the irrevocable aspect of Christ's self-gift in divinization corresponds to the indissoluble dimension of the conjugal act; and the radical aspect of Christ's self-gift in divinization corresponds to the radical aspect of mutual total self-gift of husband and wife in one flesh union, -the conjugal act.

Because the mystery of Sanctification or divinization in its irrevocable and radical dimensions corresponds to the one flesh union of man and wife, the conjugal act recalls, participates in, and anticipates or foreshadows, divinization. The *Theology of the Body* clarifies these correspondences:

> In its "spiritualization" and "divinization" in which man will participate in the resurrection, we discover –in an eschatological perspective- the same characteristics that mark the "spousal" meaning of the body; we discover them in the encounter with the mystery of the living God, which reveals itself through the face-to-face vision of him. (TOB 67.5)

In another place, the *Theology of the Body*, alluding to Eph. 3:9, says: "The analogy of spousal love allows us in some way to understand the mystery, which was hidden from ages in God and is realized in time by Christ as the love proper to a total and irrevocable gift of self by God to man in Christ." (TOB 95b.2). Further on, this insight is nuanced in consideration of the limitations of any analogy, but the analogy is also extended to take into account the revealed truth that sanctification involves a participation in God's nature. John Paul develops this idea as follows:

> The analogy of the love of spouses or spousal love seems *to emphasize* above all *the aspect of God's gift of himself to man* who is chosen "from ages" in Christ (literally, his gift of self to "Israel" to the "Church"); a gift that is in its essential character, or as gift, total (or rather "radical") and irrevocable. This gift is certainly "radical" and therefore "total." One cannot speak here of totality in the metaphysical sense. As a creature, man is in fact not capable of "receiving" the gift of God in the transcendental fullness of his divinity. Such a "total gift" (an uncreated gift) is shared only by God himself in the "trinitarian communion of persons." By contrast, God's gift of himself to man, which is what the analogy of spousal love speaks about, *can only have the form of a participation in the divine nature* (see 2 Pet 1:4) as theology has made clear with great precision. (TOB 95b.4)

III.4.2d The Conjugal Act and the Radical Character of Grace

Spousal love or the conjugal act is paradigmatic of grace by virtue of its privileged analogous penetration of the mystery of Sanctification, which is God's irrevocable and radical self-gift. Once again, respecting the limitations of any analogy, the *Theology of the Body* teaches that: "The *mystery* remains *transcendent with respect to this analogy* as with respect to any other analogy with which we try to express it in any human language. At the same time however, this analogy offers the possibility of a certain cognitive 'penetration' into the very essence of the mystery." (TOB 95b.1). The *Theology of the Body* reaffirms the legitimacy of this insight, irrespective of the limitations of analogy:

> Nevertheless, according to such a measure, the gift given by God to man in Christ is a 'total' or 'radical' gift, which is precisely what the analogy of spousal love indicates: it is in some sense "all" that God "could" give of himself to man, considering the limited faculties of man as a creature. In this way the analogy of spousal love indicates the "radical" character of Grace: the whole order of created grace. (TOB 95b.4)

III.4.2e The Conjugal Act: The Foundation of the Sacramental Order

Having identified the conjugal act as signifying the immanent Blessed Trinity by virtue of indissolubility, plurality, freedom, fruitfulness, dominion, and a communion of persons; and, having identified the conjugal act as signifying the economic Blessed Trinity by virtue of the mysteries of Creation, Redemption and Sanctification; and, having identified the conjugal act as signifying Christ's radical and irrevocable self-gift to man in the acts of Creation, Redemption and Sanctification; the *Theology of the Body* teaches that the conjugal act sacramentally signifies the foundation of the whole sacramental order:

> One can say that the visible sign of marriage "in the beginning," in as much as it is linked to the visible sign of Christ and the Church on the summit of God's

saving economy, *transposes* the eternal plan of love *into the "historical" dimension* and makes it *the foundation of the whole sacramental order.* It is a particular merit of the author of Ephesians that he brought these two signs together, making them *the single great sign*, that is, *a great sacrament (sacramentum magnum).* (TOB 95b.7)

At this point we can see that the entire teaching of Saint John Paul in the *Theology of the Body* reflects upon, deepens and illuminates revelation concerning the conjugal act. This is made clear, once again, in his summary and conclusion:

The doctrine contained in this document of the Church's contemporary teaching remains in organic relation both with the sacramentality of marriage and the whole biblical problematic of the theology of the body, which is centered on the "key words" of Christ. In some sense one can even say that all the reflections dealing with the "Redemption of the Body and the Sacramentality of Marriage" *seem* to constitute *an extensive commentary* on the doctrine contained precisely in *Humanae Vitae.* (TOB 133.2)

Summary of Part III

Part III discussed the relationship between *Humanae Vitae* and the *Theology of the Body* in the perspective of doctrine.

Part III.1.1 presented *Humanae Vitae's* doctrine as settled doctrine.

Part III.1.2 presented the *Theology of the Body* as a "document of the Church's contemporary Church teaching" (TOB 133.2), on the same subject matter as *Humanae Vitae.*

Part III.1.3 discussed doctrinal development as an historical phenomenon.

Part III.2 presented the widespread rejection of *Humanae Vitae* as an attack on the foundations of theology and presented the *Theology of the Body's* proposal in brief.

Part III.3 discussed theological strategies and philosophical techniques John Paul used to develop the vision presented in the *Theology of the Body's* proposal.

Part III.4 presented the thesis that according to the *Theology of the Body*, the conjugal act is the type, image and sign of the Blessed Trinity.

Part III.4.1 presented the conjugal act as signifying the immanent Blessed Trinity.

Part III.4.2 presented the conjugal act in its signification as a sacramental sign of the economic Blessed Trinity with subparts including: (a) the mystery of Creation; (b) the mystery of Redemption; (c) the mystery of Sanctification; (d) the mystery of Grace; and (e) as the foundation of the entire Sacramental order.

✝

PART IV

Development of Doctrine

Introduction to Part IV

Part IV of this dissertation discusses the *Theology of the Body's* conclusion reached in Part III as a development of doctrine; specifically, whether it is probable that Pope Saint John Paul II's understanding of the conjugal act in the *Theology of the Body* may be a genuine development of *Humanae Vitae's* doctrine and may open a new horizon for theological anthropology and the theology of marriage.

Part I presented background information in five subparts: Part I.1 outlined a number of anthropological proposals from the patristic to the scholastic period to illustrate the vitality and persistence of theological anthropology in tradition; Part I.2 analyzed a recent International Theological Commission (ITC) study as a contemporary expression of the natural law theory that animates the anthropology operative in *Humanae Vitae*; Part I.3 considered personalism, the main philosophical theory animating the anthropology operative in the *Theology of the Body*, and the philosophical theory that provides the foundational space for the *Theology of the Body* to deepen the anthropology of *Humanae Vitae* and develop its doctrine; Part I.4 presented ontology in the perspectives of being and truth; and Part I.5 considered the authority of different forms of papal pronouncements.

Part II presented the relationship between *Humanae Vitae* and the *Theology of the Body* as treatises. It compared and contrasted their goals, the questions they asked and sought to answer, the way they framed their questions, their methodologies, the authorities they invoked, and their characterizations of the conjugal act.

Part III established the organic continuity between *Humanae Vitae* and the *Theology of the Body* rooted in the conjugal act as their unitary subject matter. It characterized popular rejection of *Humanae Vitae's* doctrine as an attack on the body and therefore an attack on one of Christianity's basic foundations. It cited texts from the *Theology of the Body* to document its theological understanding of the relationship between the conjugal act and Christian mysteries. At length it established that the *Theology of the Body* proposes that the conjugal act is a sacramental sign of the mysteries of the Blessed Trinity, creation, redemption and sanctification, and is the foundation of the sacramental order and the order of grace.

Parts I, II and III establish the *Theology of the Body's* core proposal. Part IV considers the *Theology of the Body's* proposed understanding of the conjugal act as a development of the doctrine of *Humanae Vitae*. It considers whether it is plausible that the *Theology of the Body* is a genuine development of the doctrine of *Humanae Vitae* as the dissertation topic suggests: "Pope Saint John Paul II's Understanding of the Conjugal Act in the *Theology of the Body* as a Development of the Doctrine of *Humanae Vitae*: A New Horizon for Theological Anthropology and the Theology of Marriage." The core *Theology of the Body* proposal stated in propositional form is that: The conjugal act is a sacramental sign of the mysteries of the Blessed Trinity, Creation, Redemption and Sanctification, and is the foundation of the sacramental order and the order of grace.

We cannot predict whether a variant of this proposition may one day be promulgated as Church doctrine. If so, it would likely be in the distant future because the *Theology of the Body* and its proposal are not widely known within the Church. Nevertheless, because it is a comprehensive theological proposal, because it responds to an historical crisis, and because Saint John Paul is a formidable teacher, it is reasonable to consider

130

at least whether his proposal can be readily dismissed as a corruption of Christian doctrine. Blessed John Henry Cardinal Newman's *Essay on the Development of Christian Doctrine* identified seven tests, any one of which can disqualify a corrupt theological proposal. Part IV presents some biographical information about Newman, his theory of knowledge and an overview of his understanding of doctrine and doctrinal development. Newman's seven tests are explained and then applied to the *Theology of the Body's* proposal to see if they might serve to disqualify the *Theology of the Body's* proposal as a corruption of doctrine. Part V summarizes the thesis, states its conclusion, and suggests additional study topics.

IV.1 Newman, Biographical Information

John Henry Newman, the eldest of six children was born in London on February 21, 1801, of a middle-class banking family. He entered the Ealing School as a boarder in May, 1808, and Oxford in December, 1816, at age fifteen. About this time, he had a religious experience that he described as a profound awareness of the presence of himself and of God. This experience marked his initial conversion to the Christian faith. His response was to commit himself to serve God and he regarded celibacy as integral to that service.

At Oxford he garnered a reputation as a scholar of the first rank and on April 12, 1822, at age 21, was elected Fellow of Oriel College. In May, 1824, Newman was offered and accepted the curacy of St. Clements's Church, Oxford. On Sunday, June 13, of that year he was ordained Deacon in Christ Church. The following March, Newman was offered and accepted the position of Vice-Principal of Alban Hall and was ordained an Anglican priest in Christ Church by the Bishop of Oxford at the end of May 1825. In 1826, he gained additional prestige and economic self-sufficiency by his appointment as a Tutor of Oriel College, a position he also revered for its pastoral and academic mentoring potential. With this appointment he resigned his curacy at St. Clements' and his position at Alban Hall. In March, 1828, he was instituted as Vicar of Oxford and Rector of St. Mary's Church, a position he held until he resigned in 1843.

The sermon he preached at Oxford on February 2, 1843, was pivotal for Newman's career and pivotal for our consideration of John Paul II's proposition. Delivered on the feast of the Purification, or Presentation, the sermon was entitled *The Theory of Developments in Religious Doctrine*. It was the fifteenth and last of a series of his favorite sermons collectively called the Oxford University Sermons (OUS #15), all of which related to the theme of the relationship between faith and reason. In a letter to Mrs. J. Mosley a week prior to delivering the sermon, Newman remarked that:

> I now for twelve years have been working out a theory...I have kept to the same views and arguments for twelve years...They are not theological nor ecclesiastical, though they bear immediately on the most intimate and practical religious questions.[156]

The views and arguments expressed in the sermon certainly did bear immediately on the most intimate and practical religious questions. "The sermon would soon be developed into the full-length volume, *An Essay on the Development of Christian Doctrine*, that is a great classic of theology." [157]

IV.2 Doctrine and its Development; Oxford University Sermon #15

Newman's theology comes to us through voluminous sermons, tracts, essays and letters. He was not a systematic philosopher or theologian.

---

[156] John Henry Newman, *Letters and Correspondence of John Henry Newman*, vol. 2 (London: Longmans, Green and Co., 1890). Letter to Mrs. J. Mosley, January 5, 1843.

[157] Ian Ker, *John Henry Newman; a Biography*, vol. II (Oxford: Oxford University Press, 1990), 269.

Rather, he produced his philosophical and theological works in response to particular questions: a sermon preached on a scriptural text in the liturgy; a tract produced to support or refute a claim; an essay written on a topic in controversy; or a letter addressing the concerns of a particular person. All Newman's writings reflect his motto, *cor ad cor loquitur*, heart speaks unto heart.

Newman's key epistemological concepts, his thinking on the relationship between faith and reason, and his understanding of doctrine and its development are all presented concisely in one sermon, Oxford University Sermon #15, *The Theory of Development in Religious Doctrine*.

IV.2.a Scriptural Reference

February 2, 1843, was the Feast of the Purification, and the scriptural reference was taken from the second chapter of the Gospel of Saint Luke, Verse 19: "But Mary kept all these things and pondered them in her heart."

Why did Newman choose Mary as the exemplar of his *Theory of Developments in Religious Doctrine?* He chose Mary because she provided the perfect example of how faith and reason are properly exercised. The perfect relationship between faith and reason is given the most clear and convincing expression possible in the few gospel dramas in which Mary played a part, one of which is the drama from which the text chosen for the day was taken. She attended to reason. She pondered meanings in her heart. First, however, she fully embraced by faith what she had been given to believe. She believed in order that she might understand. This is the perfect response to the mysteries of faith and to the requirements of reason. The need for this balance pressed heavily on Newman as a believer, scholar, Churchman, reformer and controversialist. That he found the perfect model in a woman of humble estate, learning and disposition, reveals something of the intensity and humility with which he himself pondered the meaning of scripture.

IV.2.b Subject and Purpose of the Sermon

The *Theory of Developments in Religious Doctrine* though delivered as a sermon could easily be taken for a university lecture. It lasted an hour and a half. Broadly, the sermon is about the relationship between faith and reason. More narrowly, it is about how faith and reason relate in the development in Christian doctrine. It is not a pastoral sermon. It is not designed to change the behavior of his congregation or his readers. Instead it is noetic, directed to the minds of his audience. He apologizes for this early in the sermon:

> If, then, on a Day dedicated to such high contemplations as the feast which we are now celebrating, it is allowable to occupy the thoughts with a subject not of a devotional or practical nature, it will be some relief of the omission to select one in which St. Mary at least will be our example, —the use of Reason in investigating the doctrines of Faith;[158]

The sermon presents a theory. However, there is more going on in the sermon than an intellectual exercise in the development and presentation of a theory. The theory explains what doctrine is, how doctrine relates to faith, how doctrines come about historically, and what doctrine does. On another level, it is a quintessential apologetic. It is an explanation of faith. The sermon deals with all these questions notionally, theologically, exegetically, philosophically and doctrinally.

As interesting as these dimensions of the sermon are, there is another level to the sermon that addresses a deeper and more controversial question. The deeper question comes into view when we think about what it is that is driving the fascination with doctrine. The answer is that it is being

---

[158] John Henry Newman, *Fifteen Sermons, Preached before the University of Oxford*, 3rd ed., *Notre Dame Series in the Great Books* (South Bend: University of Notre Dame Press, 2003), 314.

driven by a controversy that preoccupied nineteenth century theology. This was the question of where the Church of the Apostles was to be found. One popular response was that the Church of England was the Church of the Apostles that inevitably had adapted to change. Another response was to acknowledge a need for reform to restore the Church of England to its apostolic roots. These responses did not satisfy Newman. They were not adequate because they were incomplete. The quests for a complete answer to this question absorbed his life and work at this time. He had nurtured the idea that the Church of England represented a middle ground, *a Via Media*, between the corruptions of the Church of Rome and the excesses of Protestant reforms. So, by developing his *Theory of Developments in Religious Doctrine*, Newman was addressing this deeper question. By preaching his theory as a sermon, he was inviting his audience to reflect upon the nature of the Church from the perspective of doctrine and how it develops.

If the burning question was to identify the contemporary manifestation of the Church of the Apostles, it is interesting to wonder why Newman did not address this question directly, for example, in a sermon entitled: *The History of the Church of the Apostles,* or *the History of the Church of England.* I believe the answer lies in Newman's brilliance in handling controversy. Initially, for Newman, it was a given that the Church of England was the Church of the Apostles and he believed that his theory would sustain this belief. In retrospect, however, he would recognize that he was entertaining doubts. He was acting on his ambition to reform the devotional life of the Church of England and to assert its independence from civil authority. He understood that true reform could not be achieved in the absence of a clear understanding of the relationship between faith, doctrine, ministry and worship. *The Theory of Developments in Religious Doctrine* was therefore essential to bring together all the parts and pieces of the reform puzzle, and to seize the high ground in the struggle for reform. As a skilled polemicist and controversialist, he knew the benefit of occupying the high ground in a way that played to his strengths. For example, confining his explorations to doctrine, he could neutralize sectarian passions that complicate discussions of Church history. Moreover, by addressing doctrine at a theoretical level, he could address the whole problem historically, intellectually and dispassionately. This would give him a commanding view of a battlefield on which he was preeminent. No one could contextualize the details of doctrine and heresy in all their historical dimensions as well as Newman. Few, if anyone, possessed his combined powers of intellect or persuasion.

Newman was vividly aware that a theory of doctrine and its development would have far reaching implications for the burning theological question of the day. He recognized that the trajectory of true doctrine and its proper development was a surrogate for the trajectory of the Church of the Apostles. By finding one, he knew that he would find the other. Nevertheless, if reform is what was needed, a theory of doctrine and its development was thereby required to make the history of the Christian Church intelligible. Shortly after delivery of this sermon he would devote himself to a volume on the same subject: "…a subject, indeed, far fitter for a volume than for the most extended notice which can here be given to it; but one which cannot be passed over altogether in silence in any attempt at determining the relation of Faith to Reason.[159]

The result was to be his theological classic *An Essay on the Development of Christian Doctrine*, which developed the theory in great detail from the same materials used in the sermon. The sermon conveys his foundational understanding of doctrinal development and the essay applies this understanding to actual historical doctrinal developments. The pivotal importance of the sermon and the essay to Newman's career is easy to see. Upon completion of his *Essay on the Development of Christian Doctrine* Newman requested to be received into the Catholic Church, "into what I believe to be the One-Fold of the Redeemer."[160]

---

[159] John Henry Newman, "The Theory of Developments in Religious Doctrine," in *Fifteen Sermons Preached before the University of Oxford* (South Bend: University of Notre Dame Press, 2003), 314.

[160] John Henry Newman, *A Packet of Letters*, ed. Joyce Sugg (New York: Oxford University Press, 1983), 71.

Finally, it should be pointed out that as a controversialist, Newman's consummate skill was tempered by a sustained reverence for his adversaries irrespective of their intellectual or moral vulnerability, even as he took their measure. He decided in advance what must be conceded and what must not be conceded, all while staying laser focused on the subject at hand. This permitted him to vanquish opposing arguments while retaining the love, respect and admiration of his opponents. Newman was first and always a gentleman.

IV.2.c Strategy: Christianity as an Idea

Newman weaves his theory of doctrine and its development by scrutinizing Christianity as a phenomenon, its revelation and its history, according to his epistemological understandings of knowledge by faith and knowledge by reason.

The entire sermon hinges on the notion that Christianity is an idea. Indeed, Christianity is a very big idea. Christianity as an idea undergirds the whole tapestry of the sermon. The strategy of considering Christianity as an idea allows him to explain the relationship between faith and reason and to explain doctrine as the product of reason's contemplation, or pondering, of the knowledge we have from the truths of the Christian faith.

By faith we have perfect knowledge of the whole truth of the Christian idea presented to our minds by revelation. This perfect knowledge is innate. We may or may not be able to give a good rational account of this perfect knowledge, but our knowledge of the idea is perfect and motivates us powerfully.

By reason we give an account of the idea. By reason we are able to make inferences which are true of the idea but are only partial truths and partial knowledge relative to the idea as a whole. So we have the idea of Christianity which we know perfectly by faith from revelation, and we have Christian doctrine which we know as true statements giving us

137

partial knowledge about the Christian idea by reason employed at the service of faith.

Prior to framing the question of development in the contexts of Christianity as an idea and the relation between faith and reason, Newman asserts his understanding of the Christian phenomenon as follows: "The overthrow of the wisdom of the world was one of the earliest, as well as the noblest of the triumphs of the Church"[161] This dramatic statement bids his listeners to sit up and take notice that the Christian phenomenon, the Church, not only stands over against the wisdom of the world, but it has overthrown the wisdom of the world. He asserts this as the proper context and spirit in which to understand doctrine. He immediately reinforces the intensity of this dramatic assertion:

> ...the Cross has enlisted under its banner all those great endowments of mind, which in former times had been expended on vanities, or dissipated in doubt and speculation...and...was attracting to itself all the energy, the keenness, the originality, and the eloquence of the age.[162]

Articulating the historical significance of Christianity, Newman continues: "...in the course of time the whole mind of the world, as I may say, was absorbed into the philosophy of the Cross, as the element in which it lived, and the form upon which it was molded."[163]

So Christianity is an idea that has overthrown the wisdom of the world, absorbed its energy, keenness, originality and eloquence, and has also absorbed the mind of the world into the philosophy of the Cross. For Newman, development of the Christian idea is the very meaning of history.

---

[161] Newman, "The Theory of Developments in Religious Doctrine," in *Fifteen Sermons Preached before the University of Oxford*, 314.
[162] Ibid.
[163] Ibid.

IV.2.d Epistemology

Newman's theory of knowledge undergirds his understanding of the Christian phenomenon. As we have seen, Newman understood knowledge by faith as essentially different from knowledge by reason, even if both are knowledge of the same object.

First consider the knowledge of faith. Newman explains that the Christian mysteries of the Holy Trinity and the Incarnation are objects of faith. Revelation impresses objects of faith upon the mind. These innate impressions, ideas, or visions, influence us powerfully, even when we are not conscious of them. Our faith is in these objects of faith, of which our innate impressions are genuine and perfect ideas of divinely revealed truths. This gives us what scripture knows as knowledge.

So the knowledge by faith, presented in revelation, comes to us by acts of faith, which give us the innate impressions that are genuine and perfect ideas of divinely revealed truths. A consequence of this understanding of knowledge by faith is that the knowledge by faith of the least educated peasant can exceed the knowledge by faith of the most educated theologian. This is true because reason is subordinate to faith. Newman explains:

> Reason has not only submitted, it has ministered to Faith; it has illustrated its documents; it has raised illiterate peasants into philosophers and divines.[164] In this way: 'doctrine may rather be said to use the minds of Christians, than to be used by them.'[165]

What then is knowledge by reason? Newman explains that doctrinal statements, confessions, creeds, or articles of the faith belong to knowledge by reason. They are true propositions about the objects of faith impressed

---

[164] Ibid., 317.
[165] Ibid.

upon our minds by revelation. So doctrine is knowledge by reason consisting of true propositions about objects of faith.

What then is the connection between the innate knowledge by faith of the objects of faith and doctrinal propositions? Newman explains that:

> Theological dogmas are propositions expressive of the judgments which the mind forms, or the impressions which it receives, of revealed truth. Revelation sets before it certain supernatural facts and actions, beings and principles; these make a certain impression or image upon it; and this impression spontaneously, or even necessarily, becomes the subject of reflection on the part of the mind itself, which proceeds to investigate it, and to draw it forth in successive and distinct sentences.[166]

He further explains that as we ponder these supernatural facts of revelation, we formulate rational propositions in an effort to express them:

> Particular propositions, then, which are used to express portions of the great idea vouchsafed to us, can never really be confused with the idea itself which all such propositions taken together can but reach, and cannot exceed. …the dogmatic statements of the Divine Nature used in our confessions, however multiplied, cannot say more than is implied in the original idea, considered in its completeness, without the risk of heresy. Creeds and dogmas live in the one idea which they are designed to express, and which alone is substantive; and are necessary only because the human mind cannot reflect upon that idea, except piecemeal…and in matter of fact these expressions are never equivalent to it; …thus the Catholic

---

[166] Ibid., 320.

dogmas are, after all, but symbols of a Divine fact, which, far from being compassed by those very propositions, would not be exhausted, nor fathomed, by a thousand.[167]

An analogy may help here. A ray of sunlight may be useful in describing the kind of knowledge that is provided to us by doctrinal statements. The ray of sunlight is from the sun, and is about the sun, and is true of the sun, but it is not the whole truth of the sun. What we know of a ray of sunlight can be likened to propositions that are true about objects of faith. The whole truth of the sun, which is the sun itself, can be likened to objects of faith themselves.

Newman reinforces this distinction with a simple example: "…the developments in the doctrines of the Holy Trinity and the Incarnation are mere portions of the original impression, and modes of representing it."[168] He further reinforces the idea of piecemeal portions by reminding his audience that: "When we pray, we pray, not to an assemblage of notions, or to a creed, but to One Individual Being; and, when we speak of Him, we speak of a Person, not of a Law or a Manifestation."[169]

Newman further explains that the doctrinal propositions are truths of the science of theology, and that they relate to the inward knowledge of the object of faith the way propositions in other sciences relate to the perfect truth of their subject matter. For example, Newman argues that the physical world is the subject matter and the perfect truth of the science of physics. The science of physics offers propositions about that perfect truth. However, Newman argues that the propositions offered by physics rely on foundational concepts that are not adequate to exhaust the perfect truth of the physical world. Using Ptolemaic and Copernican solar schemes, Newman argues that, though contradictory, both schemes are true relative to their different foundational concepts. He argues further

---

[167] Ibid., 331.
[168] Ibid., 330.
[169] Ibid.

that both can be true or both can be false relative to different foundational conceptions of motion. Newman gives this illustration to demonstrate that the truth of science depends upon presuppositions that are themselves vulnerable to change:

> ...it would follow that the laws of physics, as we consider them, are themselves but generalizations of economical exhibitions, inferences from figure and shadow, and not more real than the phenomena from which they are drawn. Scripture, for instance, says that the sun moves and the earth is stationary; and science, that the earth moves, and the sun is comparatively at rest. How can we determine which of these opposite statements is the very truth, till we know what motion is? If our idea of motion be but an accidental result of our present senses, neither proposition is true, and both are true; neither true philosophically, both true for certain practical purposes in the system in which they are respectively found; and physical science will have no better meaning when it says that the earth moves, than plane astronomy when it says that the earth is still.[170]

By these examples Newman establishes the integrity of the science of theology among all other sciences. Further, he shows how the propositions of theology, like the propositions of all other sciences, are economical representations of the whole truth of the science to which they belong.

IV.2.e Economical Representations

Having thus described the laws of physics as economical ways of describing phenomena that are a small part of the whole truth of physics, and are

---

[170] Ibid., 347.

either true or not true depending upon a prior choice of foundational concepts, Newman asserts that the same economies are applied in all teaching.

Newman addresses criticisms that disdain instances in which Christian stories, such as those offering details of martyrdoms, or speculations about biblical characters, are farfetched or embellished. He responds that these are often economies much like the economies utilized in the explanation of physical phenomena in the science of physics, not completely true, but sufficiently true to the purpose at hand. He reminds his hearers that all sciences do this and that all teaching and instruction is accomplished by accommodation to the cognitive capabilities of the student:

> Children, who are made our pattern in Scripture, are taught, by an accommodation, on the part of their teachers, to their immature faculties and their scanty vocabulary. To answer their questions in the language which we should use towards grown men, would be simply to mislead them, if they could construe it at all.[171]

IV.2.f How Religious Doctrine Develops

Scripture provides a framework for doctrine but leaves it unfinished, in need of pondering. Newly proclaimed articles of faith are developments of doctrine. In the process of divining these propositions, reason submits to and ministers to faith. Developments are not exclusively derived by rigorous logical deduction from prior propositions. Rather, they are always latent in the genuine and perfect impression or idea of the object of faith, and brought out by contemplation of the object of faith. As Newman states:

---

[171] Ibid., 340.

Further, I observe, that though the Christian mind reasons out a series of dogmatic statements, one from another, this it has ever done, and always must do, not from those statements taken in themselves, as logical propositions, but as being itself enlightened and (as if) inhabited by that sacred impression which is prior to them, which acts as a regulating principle, ever present, upon the reasoning, and without which no one has any warrant to reason at all.[172]

Here Newman anticipates and responds to another objection. To those who criticize the primacy given to objects of faith or to passages of scripture by the Fathers of the Church as weak reasoning, in their theological reflection, he says: "…it will account for the charge of weak reasoning commonly brought against those Fathers; for never do we seem so illogical to others as when we are arguing under the continual influence of impressions to which they are insensible."[173]

Doctrine always gives us partial knowledge about objects of faith. Our innate perfect ideas of the objects of faith perform the principal regulatory function for doctrinal development because doctrine is always latent in these ideas. Historically, heresies instigate a response which casts doctrine into new forms. Hence, heresy is often a driver of doctrinal development.

IV.2.g Music and Doctrine

Newman also uses music as an analogy to explain the relationship between doctrines and the objects of faith they represent. Newman:

Let us take another instance, of an outward and earthly form, or economy, under which great wonders unknown

[172] Ibid., 334.
[173] Ibid.

seem to be typified; I mean musical sounds, as they are exhibited most perfectly in instrumental harmony. There are seven notes in the scale; make them fourteen; yet what a slender outfit for so vast an enterprise! What science brings so much out of so little? Out of what poor elements does some great master in it create his new world! Shall we say that all this exuberant inventiveness is a mere ingenuity or trick of art, like some game or fashion of the day, without reality, without meaning? We may do so; and then, perhaps, we shall also account the science of theology to be a matter of words; yet, as there is a divinity in the theology of the Church, which those who feel cannot communicate, so is there also in the wonderful creation of sublimity and beauty of which I am speaking.[174]

Newman likens the seven musical notes to facts revelation presents as objects of faith. In themselves they are extremely limited, and Newman marvels at their ability under the guidance of a great master to create new worlds, and marvels, likewise, at the many such worlds that can be created from the partial and piecemeal material provided by seven notes.

IV.3 Newman's Seven Notes, or Tests, of Doctrinal Development

This section proceeds from Newman's Oxford University Sermon #15 to the seven tests he identified in his *Essay on the Development of Christian Doctrine*, completed two years and eight months after the sermon. The tests are listed along with a clarification of their meaning. Their operation is illustrated by excerpts from Newman's explanations and/or by combining a relevant objection with Newman's retort. The objections

---

[174] Newman, *Fifteen Sermons, Preached before the University of Oxford*, #39.

are general allegations or protests against different doctrinal developments and the retorts exemplify Newman's application of the tests.

In his multiyear laboring over the issue of doctrinal development, Newman applied the tests retrospectively to see if doctrines promulgated by the Catholic Church through history could be justified as faithful developments of the Christian idea. Or, alternatively, and this was his initial expectation, if these doctrines could be rejected as corruptions of the Christian idea. In a later section the seven tests are applied to see if they can expose, disqualify and dismiss the *Theology of the Body's* proposal as a corruption of doctrine. In that exercise, however, the tests are applied prospectively, to see if by Newman's tests the *Theology of the Body* distorts doctrine instead of being a potentially genuine development of doctrine, that increases our partial knowledge of the Christian idea.

Newman compressed all seven notes, or tests, or criteria for distinguishing corruptions of doctrine from potentially genuine developments into a single one-sentence summary. Propositions that are genuine or potentially genuine doctrinal developments meet all of these criteria:

> To guarantee its own substantial unity it must be seen to be one in type, one in its system of principles, one in its unitive power towards externals, one in its logical consecutiveness, one in the witness of its early phases to its later, one in the protection which its later extend to its earlier, and one in its union of vigor with continuance, that is, in its tenacity.[175]

Because Newman's style can be as long as it is elegant, I will attempt a shorthand version of his meaning where possible in the text, and use his actual words in the footnotes if necessary. Each of the seven tests will be explained in the following subsections beginning with Preservation of Type.

---

[175] Newman, *An Essay on the Development of Christian Doctrine.*

IV.3.a Test #1, Preservation of Type

(*It must be seen to be one in type*)

Meaning:

> ...whereas, all great ideas are found, as time goes on, to involve much which was not seen at first to belong to them, and have developments, that is enlargements, applications, uses and fortunes, very various, one security against error and perversion in the process is the maintenance of the original type, which the idea presented to the world at its origin, amid and through all its apparent changes and vicissitudes from first to last. ...Let us take it as the world now views it in its age; and let us take it as the world once viewed it in its youth; and let us see whether there be any great difference between the early and the later description of it.[176]

Challenge, Allegation or Protest:

The Catholic Church today bears no resemblance to the Church of the Patriarchs.

Newman Retorts:

> If then there is now a form of Christianity such that it extends throughout the world, though with varying measures of prominence and prosperity in separate places; that it lies under the power of sovereigns and magistrates, in various ways alien to its faith; that flourishing nations and great empires, professing or tolerating the Christian

---

[176] Ibid., 207.

name, lie over against it as antagonists; that schools of philosophy and learning are supporting theories, and following out conclusions, hostile to it, and establishing an exegetical system hostile to its Scriptures; that it has lost whole Churches by schism, and is now opposed by powerful communions once part of itself; that it has been altogether or almost driven from some countries; that in others its line of teachers is overlaid, its flocks oppressed; its Churches occupied, its property held by what may be called a duplicate succession; that in others its members are degenerate and corrupt, and are surpassed in conscientiousness and in virtue, as in gifts of intellect, by the very heretics whom it condemns; that heresies are rife and bishops negligent within its own pale; and that amid its disorders and its fears there is but one Voice for whose decisions the peoples wait with trust, one Name and one See to which they look with hope, and that name Peter, and that See Rome; such a religion is not unlike the Christianity of the fifth and sixth centuries...The above sketch has run to great length, yet, it is only part of what might be set down in evidence of the wonderful identity of type which characterizes the Catholic Church from first to last. [177]

IV.3.b Test#2, Continuity of Principles

(*It must be seen to be one in its system of principles*)

The continuity of principles test requires understanding what is meant by the principles of Christian doctrine that Newman has in mind. He

---

[177] Ibid., 321-22 and footnote.

identifies and explains nine out of many such principles, and chooses four of those to elaborate in greater detail:

> For the convenience of arrangement, I will consider the Incarnation the central truth of the gospel, and the source whence we are to draw out its principles. This great doctrine is unequivocally announced in numberless passages of the New Testament, especially by St. John and St. Paul... In such passages as these we have:

1. The principle of *dogma*[178]
2. The principal of *faith*[179]
3. The principle of *theology*[180]
4. The *sacramental* principle[181]
5. The interpretation of Scripture in a second or *mystical sense*[182]
6. The principle of *grace*[183]

---

[178] Ibid., 325. "The principle of *dogma*, that is, supernatural truths irrevocably committed to human language, imperfect because it is human, but definitive and necessary because given from above"

[179] Ibid. "The principal of *faith*, which is the correlative of dogma, being the absolute acceptance of the divine Word with an internal assent, in opposition to the informations, if such, of sight and reason."

[180] Ibid. "Faith, being an act of the intellect, opens a way for inquiry, comparison and inference, that is, for science in religion, in subservience to itself; this is the principle of *theology*.

[181] Ibid. "The doctrine of the Incarnation is the announcement of a divine gift conveyed in a material and visible medium, it being thus that heaven and earth are in the Incarnation united. That is, it establishes in the very idea of Christianity the *sacramental* principle as its characteristic."

[182] Ibid. "Another principle involved in the doctrine of the Incarnation, viewed as taught or as dogmatic, is the necessary use of language, e.g. of the text of Scripture, in a second or *mystical sense*. Words must be made to express new ideas and are invested with a sacramental office."

[183] Ibid. "It is our Lord's intention in His Incarnation to make us what He is Himself; this is the principle of *grace*, which is not only holy but sanctifying."

7. The principle of *asceticism*[184]
8. The principle of the *malignity of sin*[185]
9. The principle that matter as well as mind is *capable of sanctification*.[186]

> Here are nine specimens of Christian principles out of the many which might be enumerated, and will anyone say that they have not been retained in vigorous action in the Church at all times amid whatever development of doctrine Christianity has experienced, so as even to be the very instruments of that development, and as patent, and as operative, in the Latin and Greek Christianity of this day as they were in the beginning?[187]

Newman makes clear that doctrine in the Catholic Church has always and everywhere been guided by rigorous, if not slavish, fidelity to demanding principles that she does not abandon under the most withering circumstances of heresy or social decay. She has maintained these principles and others like them uninterruptedly in good times and in bad for two millennia. Newman continues:

> I will single out four as specimens, -Faith, Theology, Scripture, and Dogma.

---

[184] Ibid. 325 "It cannot elevate and change us without mortifying our lower nature: —here is the principle of *asceticism*."

[185] Ibid., 326. "And, involved in this death of the natural man, is necessarily a revelation of the *malignity of sin*, in corroboration of the forebodings of conscience."

[186] Ibid. "Also by the fact of an Incarnation we are taught that matter is an essential part of us, and, as well as mind, is *capable of sanctification*."

[187] Ibid.

a) The Principle of the Supremacy of Faith

Antagonistic to this is the principle that doctrines are only so far to be considered true as they are logically demonstrated. This is the assertion of Locke…he certainly holds that for an individual to act on Faith without proof, or to make Faith a personal principle of conduct for themselves, without waiting till they have got their reasons accurately drawn out and serviceable for controversy, is enthusiastic and absurd. [Locke recommends:] "… not entertaining any proposition with greater assurance than the proofs it is built upon warrant. Whoever goes beyond this measure of assent, it is plain, receives not truth … not truth for truth's sake, but for some other by-end."[188]

[Newman's response:] It does not seem to have struck him that our "by-end" may be the desire to please our Maker, and that the defect of scientific proof may be made up to our reason by our love of Him. It does not seem to have struck him that such a philosophy as his cut off from the possibility and the privilege of faith all but the educated few, all but the learned, the clear-headed, the men of practiced intellects and balanced minds, men who had leisure, who had opportunities of consulting others, and kind and wise friends to whom they deferred. How could a religion ever be Catholic, if it was to be called credulity or enthusiasm in the multitude to use those ready instruments of belief, which alone Providence had put into their power? On such philosophy as this, were it generally received, no great work ever would have

---

[188] Ibid., 327.

been done for God's glory and the welfare of man. The 'enthusiasm' against which Locke writes may do much harm, and act at times absurdly; but calculation never made a hero. However, it is not to our present purpose to examine this theory, and I have done so elsewhere. Here I have but to show the unanimity of Catholics, ancient as well as modern, in their absolute rejection of it.[189]

b) *The Principle of Theology*

In his Oxford University Sermon #15, referenced above, Newman states that reason is subservient to faith, and that Mary, because she pondered these things in her heart, is the model of theology. In his more extended essay, Newman develops the relationship between theology, a science or work of reason, and the certitude of faith:

I have spoken and have still to speak of the action of logic, implicit and explicit, as a safeguard, and thereby a note, of legitimate developments of doctrine: but I am regarding it here as that continuous tradition and habit in the Church of a scientific analysis of all revealed truth, which is an ecclesiastical principle rather than a note of any kind, as not merely bearing upon the process of development, but applying to all religious teaching equally, and which is almost unknown beyond the pale of Christendom. Reason, thus considered, is subservient to faith, as handling, examining, explaining, recording, cataloguing, defending, the truths which faith, not reason, has gained for us, as providing an intellectual expression of supernatural facts, eliciting what is implicit,

---

[189] Ibid., 328.

comparing, measuring, connecting each with each, and forming one and all into a theological system.[190]

Newman explains that the first step in theology is investigation, and that with regard to matters of faith that are professed without intelligent commitment, that: "Our Lord gives no countenance to such lightness of mind; He calls on His disciples to use their reason, and to submit it."[191] He further notes the Lord's favorable disposition toward the rational inquiries of Nathanael, Nicodemus, St. Thomas the apostle, and the centurion, in addition to Mary's inquiries and ponderings, to show that the Lord countenances the use of our reason.

c) The Principle of Scripture and its Mystical Interpretation

Newman argues that a principle of all Christian teaching is its reference to Scripture. He argues forcefully for the priority of the mystical sense in the interpretation of Scripture. And he argues that the mystical interpretation of Scripture is the Church's most subtle and powerful method of proof for the establishment of doctrines. Newman explains:

The divines of the Church are in every age engaged in regulating themselves by Scripture, appealing to Scripture in proof of their conclusions, and exhorting and teaching in the thoughts and language of Scripture. Scripture may be said to be the medium in which the mind of the Church has energized and developed.[192]

---

190 Ibid., 336.
191 Ibid., 337.
192 Ibid., 339.

Holy Scripture is so fashioned and composed by the Holy Ghost as to be accommodated to all plans, times, persons, difficulties, dangers, diseases, the expulsion of evil, the obtaining of good, the stifling of errors, the establishment of doctrines, the ingrafting of virtues, the averting of vices. Hence it is deservedly compared by St. Basil to a dispensary which supplies various medicines against every complaint. From it did the Church in the age of Martyrs draw her firmness and fortitude; in the age of Doctors, her wisdom and light of knowledge; in the time of heretics, the overthrow of error; in time of prosperity, humility and moderation; fervor and diligence, in a lukewarm time; and in times of depravity and growing abuse, reformation from corrupt living and return to the first estate.[193]

He, then, who thinks he can tear away Scholastic Science from the work of commenting on Holy Scripture is hoping for offspring without a mother.[194]

Her most subtle and powerful method of proof, whether in ancient or modern times, is the mystical sense, which is so frequently used in doctrinal controversy as on many occasions to supersede any other.[195]

It may be almost laid down as an historical fact, that the mystical interpretation and orthodoxy will stand or fall together.[196]

---

[193] Ibid., 341. (Opp. t. i. p. 9)
[194] Ibid., 342. (Proem. 5.)
[195] Ibid.
[196] Ibid., 344.

The use of Scripture then, especially its spiritual or second sense, as a medium of thought and deduction, is a characteristic principle of doctrinal teaching in the Church.[197]

d) The Principle of Dogma

Christian discipleship means witnessing to the truth. Without the principle of dogma, the truth to which Christians were to bear witness would be indefinite, informal and would vary with each believer. On the contrary: "Christians were bound to defend and transmit the faith which they had received, and they received it from the rulers of the Church; and on the other hand it was the duty of those rulers to watch over and define this traditionary faith."[198] The Church's consistency and thoroughness in teaching is another aspect of the same principle, and "no government was ever more consistent and systematic than that of the Romish Church."[199]

Newman argues that, by virtue of the continuity of principles, theologians who would wish to strike down a doctrine as an innovation would have to show a discontinuity in the principles applied to the doctrinal development "...for instance, that the right of private judgment was secured to the early Church and has been lost to the latter, or, again, that the later Church rationalizes and the earlier went by faith."[200]

---

[197] Ibid., 346.
[198] Ibid., 348.
[199] Ibid., 352.
[200] Ibid., 353.

The integrity of the continuity of principles is further emphasized in Newman's attack on Protestantism on that very point. He says: "...the contempt of mystery, of reverence, of devoutness, of sanctity, are other notes of the heretical spirit. As to Protestantism, it is plain in how many ways it has reversed the principles of Catholic Theology."[201]

IV.3.c Test #3, Power of Assimilation

(*It must be seen to be one in its unitive power towards externals*)

Meaning:

In the physical world, whatever has life is characterized by growth, so that in no respect to grow is to cease to live. It grows by taking into its own substance external materials; and this absorption or assimilation is completed when the materials appropriated come to belong to it or enter into its unity. Two things cannot become one, except there be a power of assimilation in one or the other. Sometimes assimilation is effected only with an effort; it is possible to die of repletion, and there are animals who lie torpid for a time under the contest between the foreign substance and the assimilating power. And different food is proper for different recipients. This analogy may be taken to illustrate certain peculiarities in the growth or development in ideas...[202]

---

[201] Ibid., 354.
[202] Ibid., 185-6.

Challenge, Allegation or Protest:

"That truth and falsehood in religion are but a matter of opinion; that one doctrine is as good as another; …that no one is answerable for his opinions."[203]

Newman Retorts:

> Such was the conflict of Christianity with… Paganism…Oriental Mysteries…Gnostics… Neoplatonists…Maniches…Eusebians… Arians… Montanists …Novatians, who shrank from the Catholic doctrine, without power to propagate their own. These sects had no stay or consistence, yet they contained elements of truth amid their error, and had Christianity been as they, it might have resolved into them; but it had that hold of the truth which gave its teaching a gravity, a directness, a consistency, a sternness, and a force, to which its rivals for the most part were strangers. It could not call evil good, or good evil, because it discerned the difference between them; it could not make light of what was so solemn, or desert what was so solid. Hence, in the collision, it broke in pieces its antagonists, and divided the spoils.[204]

IV.3.d Test #4, Logical Sequence

(*It must be seen to be one in its logical consecutiveness*)

---

[203] Ibid., 357.
[204] Ibid., 358-9.

Meaning:

> Logic is the organization of thought, and, as being such, is a security for the faithfulness of intellectual developments; and the necessity of using it is undeniable as far as this, that its rules must not be transgressed. That it is not brought into exercise in every instance of doctrinal development is owing to the varieties of mental constitution, whether in communities or in individuals, with whom great truths or seeming truths are lodged. The question indeed may be asked whether a development can be other in any case than a logical operation; but, if by this is meant a conscious reasoning from premises to conclusion, of course the answer must be in the negative.[205]…Accordingly it will include any progress of the mind from one judgment to another, as, for instance, by way of moral fitness which may not admit of analysis into premise and conclusion.[206]

Challenge, Allegation or Protest:

Since we profess one Baptism for the forgiveness of sins, why do we need the elaborate regimen of Confession, Absolution, Penance, Purgatory etc.?

Newman Retorts:

> Its [Baptism's] distinguishing gift…was the plenary forgiveness of sins past…. The question immediately followed, how, since there was "but one baptism for the remission of sins," the guilt of such sin was to be removed as was incurred after its administration. There must be

---

[205] Ibid., 189.
[206] Ibid., 383.

some provision in the revealed system for so obvious a need.[207]

Newman sums up his response to the controversy: "When then an answer had to be made to the question, how is post-baptismal sin to be remitted, there was an abundance of passages in scripture to make easy to the faith of the inquirer the definitive decision of the Church."[208]

IV.3.e Test #5, Anticipation of its Future

(It must be seen to be one in the witness of its early phases to its later)

Meaning:

> Since, when an idea is living, that is, influential and effective, it is sure to develop according to its own nature, and the tendencies, which are carried out on the long run, may under favorable circumstances show themselves early as well as late, and logic is the same in all ages, instances of a development which is to come, though vague and isolated, may occur from the very first, though a lapse of time be necessary to bring them to perfection. And since developments are in great measure only aspects of the idea from which they proceed, and all of them are natural consequences of it, it is often a matter of accident in what (Anselm) order they are carried out in individual minds; and it is in no wise strange that here and there definite specimens of advanced teaching should very early occur, which in the historical course are not found till a late day. The fact, then, of such early or recurring intimations of

---

[207] Ibid., 384.
[208] Ibid., 393.

tendencies which afterwards are fully realized, is a sort of evidence that those later and more systematic fulfillments are only in accordance with the original idea.[209]

Challenge, Allegation or Protest:

"… a special stumbling block and subject of scoffing [is] devotions… toward bones, blood, the heart, the hair, bits of clothes, scapulars, cords, medals, beads and the like and the miraculous powers which they often ascribe to them."[210]

Newman Retorts:

> Christianity began by considering Matter as a creature of God, and in itself 'very good.' It taught that the Highest in that flesh died on the cross…had risen again in that flesh, and had carried that flesh with Him into heaven, and that from that flesh, glorified and deified in Him, He never would be divided. As a first consequence of these awful doctrines comes that of the resurrection of the bodies of His saints, and their future glorification with Him; next, that of the sanctity of their relics;[211]

IV.3.f Test #6, Conservative Action upon its Past

(*It must be seen as one in the protection which its later enunciation extends to its earlier*)

---

[209] Ibid., 195.
[210] Ibid., 401.
[211] Ibid. p.401 - 402

Meaning:

> As developments which are preceded by definite
> indications have a fair presumption in their favor, so
> those which do but contradict and reverse the course
> of doctrine which has been developed before them, and
> out of which they spring, are certainly corrupt; for a
> corruption is a development in that very stage in which it
> ceases to illustrate, and begins to disturb, the acquisitions
> gained in its previous history.[212]

Challenge, Allegation or Protest:

The Catholic Church has invented devotions to litanies of saints and
particularly to St. Mary with the result that worship of Jesus Christ is
dissipated and weakened.

Newman Retorts:

> And if we take a survey of at least Europe, we shall
> find that it is not those religious communions which
> are characterized by devotion toward the Blessed Virgin
> that have ceased to adore her Eternal Son but those very
> bodies which have renounced devotion to her.[213]

IV.3.g Test #7, Chronic Vigor

*(It must be seen to be one in its union of vigor with continuance, that is, in
its tenacity)*

---

[212] Ibid., 199.
[213] Ibid., 426.

Meaning:

> We have arrived at length at the seventh and last test,
> which was laid down when we started, for distinguishing
> the true development of an idea from its corruptions and
> perversions: it is this. A corruption, if vigorous, is of brief
> duration, runs itself out quickly, and ends in death; on
> the other hand, if it lasts, it fails in vigor and passes into
> a decay. This general law gives us additional assistance
> in determining the character of the developments of
> Christianity commonly called Catholic.[214]

Challenge, Allegation or Protest:

"The theology of St. Thomas, nay of the Church of his period, is built
on that very Aristotelianism, which the early Fathers denounce as the
source of all mis-belief, and in particular of the Arian and Monophysite
heresies."[215]

Newman Retorts:

> Indeed it is one of the most popular charges against the
> Catholic Church that she is 'incorrigible;'-change she
> cannot, if we listen to St. Athanasius or St. Leo; change
> she never will, if we believe the controversialist or alarmist
> of the present day."[216] In another place Newman famously
> says: "In a higher world it is otherwise, but here below
> to live is to change, and to be perfect is to have changed
> often."[217]

---

[214] Ibid., 437.
[215] Ibid., 443.
[216] Ibid., 444.
[217] Ibid., 40.

IV.4 Newman's Seven Tests and the *Theology of the Body*

This section considers the question of whether the *Theology of the Body* develops the doctrine of *Humanae Vitae*, or more correctly, whether it can be disqualified as a development of doctrine according to the seven tests of genuine doctrinal developments provided by Blessed John Henry Newman as outlined in the preceding section. Specifically, this section considers whether the *Theology of the Body's* proposition, that the conjugal act is a sacramental sign of the mysteries of the Blessed Trinity, of Creation, of Redemption, of Sanctification, and is the foundation of the sacramental order and the order of grace, deepens the explanation of the Christian truth in this area and offers a new horizon for theological anthropology and the theology of marriage. Once again, we will consider Newman's seven tests.

IV.4.a The *Theology of the Body* and Preservation of Type

(It must be seen to be one in type.)

Would consideration of the proposition as doctrine alter the idea of Christianity so that it would no longer be the same idea it was formerly because of the addition of this doctrine? At issue is the unity and identity of the Christian idea with itself through a stage in which John Paul's proposal were to become Church doctrine. Would the adoption of John Paul's proposal change the idea of Christianity?

Recognizing that the proposition has a profound effect on the way theology relates the conjugal act to fundamental Christian mysteries, to grace and to the sacraments, I would argue that its principal effect is a deepening of the Church's theological understanding of Christian truth in this area. While it affects the way theology explains the conjugal act and fundamental Christian mysteries, it does so in a way that is accretive to, and not reductive of, antecedent theological explanations. Therefore, while it may have profound effects in terms of the intelligibility of Christian mysteries on the Church's self-understanding, on pastoral and catechetical approaches, and on more, the Christian idea as such would be unaffected, remaining identical to itself before and after the proposed development. For this reason I would argue the proposal cannot be disqualified on the basis of Preservation of Type.

IV.4.b The *Theology of the Body* and Continuity of Principles

(*It must be seen to be one in its system of principles.*)

According to Newman: "...doctrines grow and are enlarged, principles are permanent;"[218] and, "doctrines are developed by the operation of principles, and develop variously according to those principles."[219]

We shall consider John Paul's proposition in the perspective of those principles of Christian doctrines Newman identified. Our interest is in whether the proposed development can be disqualified on the basis of not being in continuity with any of those principles.

The Dogmatic Principle

The first is the dogmatic principle whereby some supernatural truths are irrevocably committed to definitive human language. The dogmatic principle is unaffected by John Paul's proposition. The proposition merely develops the anagogic dimension of an established moral doctrine. It is neither in continuity nor discontinuity with the dogmatic principle. Theological proposals that contradict or diminish dogmatic statements run afoul of the dogmatic principle and that is not the case. There is no hint of a contradiction or diminution of a dogmatic statement in

---

[218] Ibid., 178.
[219] Ibid., 180.

Theology of the Body. To the extent that Manichean demons influence theological understanding of sexuality, there is a hurdle to be scaled. To that tendency, George Weigel has said: "John Paul's may prove to be the decisive moment in exorcizing the Manichaean demon and its deprecation of human sexuality from Catholic moral theology."[220]

However, neither can we say that it is in continuity with dogmatic statements. While it does not contradict them, it cannot be said definitively, that is dogmatically, that the proposition at hand is in continuity with dogma. Therein lays the tension that inheres in theology. Doctrine, Newman reminds us, gives us partial truths about objects of faith and only faith gives us certain knowledge of faith's objects. So as we strive to understand partial truths about the mysteries of Christianity, the proposition at hand, as an entrant into the doctrinal patrimony of the Church, will rise or fall according to its cogency for true believers, the *sensus fidelium.*[221] Theological speculations may become dogmatic statements when formally defined as such by the teaching authority of the Church. For example, the Assumption of the Blessed Virgin Mary into Heaven may have been theological speculation that became doctrine as it was embraced by the faithful and ultimately was infallibly defined

---

[220] Weigel, 342.

[221] Various, *Sensus Fidei in the Life of the Church* (Rome: International Theological Commission, 2014), http://www.vatican.va/roman_curia/congregations/cfaith/cti_documents/rc_cti_20140610_sensus-fidei_en.html. "In matters of faith the baptized cannot be passive. They have received the Spirit and are endowed as members of the body of the Lord with gifts and charisms 'for the renewal and building up of the Church', so the magisterium has to be attentive to the *sensus fidelium*, the living voice of the people of God. Not only do they have the right to be heard, but their reaction to what is proposed as belonging to the faith of the Apostles must be taken very seriously, because it is by the Church as a whole that the apostolic faith is borne in the power of the Spirit. The magisterium does not have sole responsibility for it. The magisterium should therefore refer to the sense of faith of the Church as a whole. The *sensus fidelium* can be an important factor in the development of doctrine, and it follows that the magisterium needs means by which to consult the faithful."

as dogma by the magisterium in concert with the *sensus fidelium*, in the mid-20th century.

The Primacy of Faith Principle

The second principle is the primacy of faith principle which requires absolute acceptance and internal assent to the divine Word even as it may be in opposition to our vision or our reason. John Paul's proposition theologically develops the anthropological foundation of a moral doctrine. Whether the moral doctrine requires the assent of faith is a prior and controverted question. John Paul's proposal understands the moral doctrine to be grounded in revelation and sacred tradition and to require the assent of faith. His proposed development of the anagogic dimension of the moral doctrine is a catechesis of the ordinary magisterium which John Paul grounds in revelation. John Paul understood the moral doctrine to require the assent of faith. Our concern is with the principle of the primacy of faith and how this principle would be affected by the recognition of John Paul's proposal as a genuine development of doctrine. The principle would be unaffected by such a development of doctrine because the doctrine would in that event require the assent of faith. The *Theology of the Body's* proposal is therefore in continuity with the principle of the primacy of faith.

The Theological Principle

The third is the theological principle which opens the way for science to inquire into religion, in Anselm's phrase, for faith to seek understanding. In as much as John Paul's proposition is a theological search for a deeper understanding of a moral doctrine, it is in continuity with the theological principle.

166

The Sacramental Principle

The fourth is the sacramental principle. As noted above: "The doctrine of the Incarnation is the announcement of a divine gift conveyed in a material and visible medium, it being thus that heaven and earth are in the Incarnation united. That is, it establishes in the very idea of Christianity the *sacramental* principle as its characteristic."[222] John Paul's proposed proposition is sacramental in its internal structure, and therefore is in continuity with Christianity's sacramental principle.

The Mystical Principle

The fifth is the mystical principle whereby: "Words must be made to express new ideas, and are invested with a sacramental office."[223] Continuity with the mystical principle is operative in John Paul's proposition in many ways. He develops the dogmatic understanding of the term 'person' which, in its mystical sense, derives from the dogmatic definitions of the Blessed Trinity and the Hypostatic Union. As noted in Part I.3, these mystical definitions bequeathed a new anthropological understanding to philosophy. John Paul's proposition further develops the mystical sense of the term 'person.' He enriches the term by including within its compass a sacramental connection between the language of the body and the sublime Christian mysteries of the Blessed Trinity and the hypostatic union, which gave us our contemporary understanding of the term. This inaugurated what has come to be commonly referred to as the nuptial mystery. In this and other ways the *Theology of the Body* is inherently mystical and in continuity with the mystical principle.

---

[222] Newman, *An Essay on the Development of Christian Doctrine*, 325.
[223] Ibid.

The Principle of Grace

The sixth is the principle of grace. Newman: "It is Our Lord's intention in his Incarnation to make us what he is himself; this is the principle of grace which is not only holy but sanctifying."[224] John Paul's proposition that the conjugal act is foundational to the sacramental order and the order of grace is in continuity with the principle of grace.

The Principle of Asceticism

The seventh is the principle of asceticism which holds that we cannot be elevated and changed without mortifying our lower nature[225]. John Paul's proposition and the moral doctrine of *Humanae Vitae* which it proposes to develop are in continuity with the ascetic principle and both explicitly identify ascetic practice as integral to a correct sacramental understanding of the conjugal act. In this way John Paul's proposition is in continuity with the principle of asceticism.

The Principle of the Malignity of Sin

The eighth is the principle of the malignity of sin. John Paul's proposition is in continuity with this Christian principle. It makes clear that the language of the body calls us to a sacramental understanding of the body and to the avoidance of a lustful understanding of the body which leads to sin. The *Theology of the Body* comports with the moral imperative of *Humanae Vitae* and avers that we are called to live according to the sacramentality spoken by the language of the body. The *Theology of the Body* calls for a response of turning away from the malignity of sin

---

224 Ibid.

225 Ibid.

including the violation of *Humanae Vitae's* moral imperative that John Paul's proposition proposes to develop.

The Principle of Sanctification

The ninth is the principle of sanctification. John Paul's proposition is in continuity with the Christian principle of sanctification as it proposes a deepening of the theological understanding of *theosis*, divinization, or sanctification. To repeat: "It is Our Lord's intention in his Incarnation to make us what he is himself; this is the principle of grace which is not only holy but sanctifying."[226]

IV.4.c The *Theology of the Body* and Power of Assimilation

(It must be seen to be one in its unitive power towards externals.)

The question is whether John Paul's doctrine may conflict with the body of Christian doctrine or if it assimilates with the existing body of doctrine.

While John Paul's proposition bids us to accept a theological understanding of the conjugal act involving heretofore hidden or vaguely recognized affinities between the conjugal act and foundational Christian mysteries, it does not oppose prior doctrinal understandings. There is neither conflict with traditional doctrine nor the syncretism of adding a different doctrine. Instead there is an elucidating and development of traditional doctrine brought to light by unpacking Scripture according to the catalytic hermeneutics of person and gift. The resulting relationship between John Paul's proposition and traditional doctrinal formulae is symbiotic, mutually enriching, seamlessly assimilative and portending of synthesis.

---

[226] Ibid., 326.

IV.4.d The *Theology of the Body* and Logical Sequence

(*One in its logical consecutiveness.*)

Logic is understood in a broad sense as organized thought not in the sense of formal logic. As regards John Paul's proposal, for example, the question[s] would be: is it logical that after widespread apostasy from a constant Church teaching, as experienced after the promulgation of *Humanae Vitae*, and with mounting empirical evidence of deleterious social consequences predicted by the encyclical, that a deep theological investigation is to be expected? Or, in an era that denies sexual difference as a given and substitutes a concept of gender choice and an ever-growing number of gender options, is it logical that Christianity would see itself as under siege and respond with a deepening of the truth and meaning of sexual difference? Again, de Lubac: "If you are to meet the strategic demands of the situation, and if you are to be rational in retaining what others reject, the whole matter has to be studied from a new viewpoint."[227]

Suspending for a moment the merits of the proposed development, it is clear that there is a logical sequence at work in the unfolding of these historical events that satisfies the test of logical sequence.

IV.4.e The *Theology of the Body* and Anticipation of the Future

(*One in the witness of its early phases to its later.*)

The question is whether John Paul's proposed doctrine can claim to be heir to a Church tradition associating conjugal acts with the foundational mysteries of Christianity. This raises two questions.

First, can it be said that there is, in the history of theology, an anticipation of John Paul's proposition as a development of doctrine? This is an easy question to answer in the affirmative. Scripture is rife

---

[227] de Lubac, 4.

with marital imagery. It begins with the marriage of Adam and Eve and ends with the wedding feast of the Lamb. In the middle, Christ begins his public ministry at a wedding and the facts of his sacrifice on Calvary, Resurrection and Ascension are generally explained in terms of nuptial consummation between heaven and earth, between the Bridegroom and the Church. Moreover, theology has a rich heritage of trying to understand the relationship between marriage and family and the divine love in the Blessed Trinity. Theology, since Paul, has extolled marriage as signifying Christ's love for the Church. So, to answer this question in the affirmative, we have only to stand back and consider the conjugal act as essential to marriage and family. In doing so we discover that associating marriage and family with the mysteries of salvation has persisted throughout Church history. It is the constant theme of theological anthropology illustrated in Part I.1. John Paul's proposal is the result of considering this perennial question afresh, and to consider it in response to an historical impetus, an apostasy, a crisis, in the heretical fallout occasioned by *Humanae Vitae's* reaffirmation of the Church's constant magisterial moral doctrine.

Newman taught that such historical occasions can have these kinds of doctrinal consequences:

> Wonderful, to see how heresy has but thrown that idea into fresh forms, and drawn out from it farther developments, with an exuberance which exceeded all questioning, and a harmony which baffled all criticism, like Him, its Divine Author, who, when put on trial by the Evil One, was but fortified by the assault, and is ever justified in His sayings, and overcomes when He is judged[228]

The second question is more speculative: what does John Paul's proposition portend for the future of the Church and for salvation history?

---

[228] Newman, *Fifteen Sermons, Preached before the University of Oxford.*

171

This is less easy to answer. However, inasmuch as marriage and family are widely recognized to be under siege in contemporary societies, and particularly in Western Christendom, the prognosis would seem to be good. John Paul's proposal elevates the theology of marriage beyond the vagaries of metaphoric or analogical representations of divine love. It raises marriage to the level of a sacramental sign of divine love *ad intra*, the immanent Blessed Trinity, and *ad extra*, the economic Blessed Trinity. It sees the conjugal act as sacramentally signifying the foundation of all sacraments and all grace. It also sees conjugal acts as sacramentally signifying the mysteries of Creation, Redemption and Sanctification. All this is seen as sacramentally accessible to us through the most intimate of human loves. It is an understanding that not only makes the Church's prohibition of contraception more intelligible; it likewise makes the indissolubility of marriage more intelligible. In addition, the *Theology of the Body* proposes that marriage is primordially sacramental; that it was created in pre-history, before the Fall, to image the Blessed Trinity, and that it was transposed into history by Christ's Redemption as the Sacrament of Matrimony and the *magnum mysterium* (Eph. 5:32). This understanding is hopeful for Christians and for the unbaptized. Greater intelligibility of Christian mysteries is greater intelligibility of the Gospel. It ignites revival, renewal, and energetic evangelization. The *Theology of the Body's* radically increased intelligibility of the good news is extraordinarily good.

IV.4.f The *Theology of the Body* and Conservative Action on the Past

(*One in the protection which its later enunciation extends to its earlier.*)

The question of whether John Paul's theological proposition conserves established doctrine requires a two-part answer.

First, the theological elevation of conjugal love conserves *Humanae Vitae's* moral prohibition of contraception because the proposed understanding increases reverence for conjugal acts.

Second, proposing the conjugal act is a sacrament of the mysteries of the Blessed Trinity, Incarnation, Creation, Redemption and Sanctification, raises a different question. Does John Paul's proposal go too far? Does catapulting the conjugal act into the stratosphere of Christian mysteries conserve or blaspheme? This question is more dangerous but offers a great opportunity. The danger is that if it is reductive of the mysteries, the proposal fails. The opportunity is that if the proposition is not reductive of the mysteries, it would not only act conservatively upon the past, but it would clearly open a new horizon for theological anthropology and the theology of marriage.

Traditional dogmas and doctrinal statements explain Christianity's highest mysteries in terms that are at some remove from conjugal acts. Why go there? Because the crisis of faith, or the heresy, is precisely about the conjugal act. *Humanae Vitae* is about the conjugal act. John Paul did not have the option to be a step removed from conjugal acts. No couching of the fundamental issue in higher levels of discourse would elucidate the theological anthropology that had to be explicated. The need for a rock-solid argument left no room for euphemism. References to conjugal acts are as elegant, measured and reverent as they are unmistakable.

Moreover, as Newman taught, there is a difference between the knowledge of the Christian idea known by faith, and the theological knowledge which gives partial truths. John Paul's proposition illuminates, broadens and deepens our partial knowledge of Christian mysteries. It throws light on the lofty mysteries but throws more light on the dignity of the human person. It teaches us that by his sexuality the human person is capacitated to be a sacrament of the highest mysteries and a witness to them. The worth of John Paul's contribution turns on these questions. Rather than being reductive of Christian mysteries, conjugal love as a sacramental sign of the Christian mysteries is accretive to human dignity and to the intelligibility of the mysteries. The *Theology of the*

Body warrants a reordering of the way we think about anthropology and marriage. It opens new theological horizons for both.

IV.4.g The *Theology of the Body* and Chronic Vigor

(One in its union of vigor with continuance, that is, in its tenacity.)

Can John Paul's proposed doctrine claim to be a persistent theme in Christian theology? Is there a theme of associating conjugal acts with the immanent Blessed Trinity, the economic Blessed Trinity, the mysteries of Creation, Redemption, Sanctification, and with the sacramental order and the order of grace?

To answer this question, we have to look back at Part I.1 on theological anthropology. There we see a small sample of theological anthropologies in Church history. Age after age, we find explanations of the creation of man and woman in the image and likeness of God and answers to the question of why God chose sexual differentiation and marriage in creating the human race. Marriage was seen by Gregory of Nyssa as consolation for the Fall's penalty of death. Marriage was seen by Athanasius as having survived the Fall without corruption. Scholars have shown that the question of whether the family was the image of God, and analogous to the Blessed Trinity, was debated in Syria as far back as the second century. Augustine and Aquinas both took up the question of the family as an image of the Blessed Trinity, which both rejected, albeit with different methodologies, goals and epistemologies.

The point to be made is that the question of sexual differentiation and marriage has vexed theology from the beginning. This may appear to be a different question from the question of whether conjugal acts are sacramental signs of the Blessed Trinity, but it is not. Conjugal acts in the Church's understanding are acts of sexual intercourse between husbands and wives indissolubly bound by their exclusive irrevocable consent and open to the generation of new life. The conjugal act in this understanding is the *sine qua non* of marriage and family. John Paul's proposal springs from a fresh consideration of the question. He comes at the question from a unique perspective. He considers marriage and family as the image of God at the level of the conjugal act. He does so because history visited an assault and a crisis upon the Church that specifically dictated the necessity of a deeper theological understanding of the conjugal act. Therefore, to say the *Theology of the Body's* proposal can lay claim to the long history of theological anthropology in which the question of whether the family is an image of God is an altogether defensible claim. Hence, we can say that John Paul's proposal meets Newman's seventh test, -one in its union of vigor with continuance, that is, its tenacity.

Further, Newman notes that:

> The absence, or partial absence, or incompleteness of dogmatic statements is no proof of the absence of impressions or implicit judgments, in the mind of the Church. Even centuries might pass without the formal expression of a truth, which had been all along the secret life of millions of faithful souls.[229]

As Newman taught with many examples throughout his *Essay on the Development of Christian Doctrine*, there is a nexus between crises or heresies and developments of doctrine.

I conclude that none of Newman's seven tests serves as a basis for disqualifying John Paul's proposition as a genuine development of doctrine.

Summary of Part IV

The introduction to Part IV summarized Parts I – III and restated John Paul's proposal as a proposition. Then it introduced Saint John Henry

---

[229] Ibid.#13

Newman with a few biographical facts about his Anglican period. It presented a sermon he preached on the topic of doctrine and doctrinal development. It analyzed the sermon, his theory of doctrinal development, and his theory of knowledge. Having preached the sermon, Newman spent the next couple of years testing his theory of development by applying it to the actual history of Catholic doctrine. While initially he intended to satisfy himself that the Catholic Church had introduced innovations or corruptions into Christian doctrine for which Anglicanism represented a remedy, his analyses, published as *An Essay on the Development of Christian Doctrine*, convinced him otherwise.

In the essay Newman identified seven tests of doctrinal developments. These tests do not guarantee that a proposed development is genuine. Instead, they present characteristics of developments that must be present to qualify them for consideration as genuine. They can, therefore, be used to disqualify any proposed development that fails one of the seven tests. These seven tests are presented and explained using examples of how Newman applied them. Then the seven tests are applied to John Paul's proposal, prospectively. This analysis concluded that none of the seven tests disqualifies John Paul's proposal.

+

PART V

Summary and Conclusion

V.1 Summary

With no diminution of *Humanae Vitae's* cosmological natural law reasoning, John Paul pursued an exegesis of scripture by phenomenological analyses using personalist subjective criteria in his *Theology of the Body* proposal. These analyses and criteria yielded deep theological insights into the conjugal act supplementing those derived by the more objective and deontological analyses of *Humanae Vitae*. Naturalistic exegeses and analyses account for mystical insights as supernatural. They reach beyond themselves to give an account of mystical realities. Personalistic exegeses and analyses, on the other hand, account for mystical realities seamlessly. They are at home in the mystical dimension because the very notion we have of person derives from the mystical, dogmatic, Trinitarian theology of the immanent Blessed Trinity of the Council of Nicaea in 325 AD, and the Christological theology of the hypostatic union of two natures in one divine person of the Council of Chalcedon in 451 AD. The *Theology of the Body* pursues personalistic and mystical understandings of the conjugal act, step by step, to a point that justifies the present investigation.

177

Part I of the dissertation introduced theological anthropology, natural law, personalism, ontology and the authority of papal pronouncements. These are principal themes operative in *Humanae Vitae* and the *Theology of the Body*.

Part II considered the historical relationship between the two teachings and compared them in specific categories. It compared the goals of *Humanae Vitae* and the *Theology of the Body*. It compared framing of the theological questions they asked to meet their respective goals. It compared the theological methodology and the authorities invoked by *Humanae Vitae* and the *Theology of the Body*. Then it compared the conjugal act as characterized by *Humanae Vitae* and by the *Theology of the Body*. It summarized these differences and clarified how, despite their differences, the *Theology of the Body* is nevertheless in continuity with *Humanae Vitae*. It established the organic and homogeneous continuity between *Humanae Vitae* and the *Theology of the Body* irrespective of their different: goals; framing of questions; methodologies; invocations of authorities; hermeneutics; and, characterizations of the conjugal act

Part III of the dissertation showed that, despite the many differences between the two documents, they were in theological and doctrinal continuity and that the *Theology of the Body* proposed a development of the doctrine of *Humanae Vitae*, or in Newman's phrase, proposed to bring aspects of the idea into consistency and form. It showed that John Paul proposed a radical understanding of the conjugal act as primordially sacramental and that it is a sacramental sign of the mysteries of the Blessed Trinity, creation, redemption and sanctification, and the foundation of the sacramental order and the order of grace.

Part IV introduced Saint John Henry Cardinal Newman, his understanding of knowledge by faith and knowledge by reason, his theory of doctrine and how Christian doctrines develop. It introduced Newman's seven tests for exposing corruptions of doctrine and disqualifying them as errant proposals that cannot be genuine doctrinal developments. It applied the seven tests to see if they could disqualify John Paul's radical theological proposal. It concluded that John Paul's proposal could not be disqualified or dismissed on the basis of Newman's seven tests of genuine doctrinal development.

V.2 Conclusion

The questions raised by the topic of this dissertation include:

- Does the *Theology of the Body* propose a new theological concept of the conjugal act?
- Does the *Theology of the Body* propose to develop the doctrine of *Humanae Vitae*?
- Does the *Theology of the Body* propose a new horizon for theological anthropology?
- Does the *Theology of the Body* propose a new horizon for the theology of marriage?
- Does the *Theology of the Body's* proposal have consequences for theology as a whole? and,
- Does the *Theology of the Body's* proposed development of *Humanae Vitae* portend development of Christian doctrine above and beyond *Humanae Vitae*?

I conclude that the answer to the first question is yes; John Paul's *Theology of the Body* proposes a new theological concept of the conjugal act. He proposes that we should understand the conjugal act theologically as a sacramental sign of the mysteries of the Blessed Trinity, of Creation, of Redemption, and of Sanctification, and as the foundation of the sacramental order and the order of grace. Understanding the conjugal act to sacramentally signify these fundamental Christian mysteries justifies recognition of John Paul's understanding as a new theological concept of the conjugal act.

I conclude that the answer to the second question is yes; John Paul's *Theology of the Body* proposes to develop *Humanae Vitae's* doctrine.

Humanae Vitae's doctrine is a moral doctrine. John Paul proposes no change to the moral doctrine. However, he does propose to develop the theological understanding of the subject of the moral doctrine which is the conjugal act. *Humanae Vitae* and the *Theology of the Body* consider the conjugal act in its natural and sacramental dimensions. However, comparing of the sacramental dimension of the conjugal act as understood by John Paul in the *Theology of the Body* to Paul VI' understanding of its sacramental dimension in *Humanae Vitae* clearly shows development. *Humanae Vitae's* understanding does not propose the sacramental signification of the conjugal act to include: the origin of holiness (see: Part II.1d.ii.a, above); nor, the Christian mysteries of the Blessed Trinity, Creation, Redemption, and Sanctification; nor, the foundation of the entire sacramental order and the order of grace. Development is unquestionable; whether it is genuine doctrinal development awaits history's verdict as it works its way from the implicit to the explicit consciousness of the Church.

I conclude that the answer to the third question is yes; John Paul's *Theology of the Body* proposes a new horizon for theological anthropology. Just as John Paul's concept of the conjugal act proposes a development of *Humanae Vitae's* doctrine, it also proposes a development of theological anthropology. John Paul's *Theology of the Body* explicitly identifies the need, and calls for an adequate theological anthropology. He responds directly to that need with his proposed concept of the conjugal act. He proposes that the conjugal act, understood as total, irrevocable, mutual, fruitful, reciprocal, self-giving of man and woman, is our beginning, our origin and our anthropological foundation. This understanding of the conjugal act proposes a new foundation and horizon for theological anthropology.

I conclude that the answer to the fourth question is yes; the *Theology of the Body* proposes a new horizon for the theology of marriage. Just as John Paul's concept of the conjugal act proposes a development of *Humanae Vitae's* doctrine, and a new horizon for theological anthropology, so also does it propose a new horizon for the theology of marriage. John Paul proposes to develop the sacramentality of marriage by developing the mystical and anagogic dimensions of the conjugal act. In developing these sacramental dimensions of the conjugal act, it develops and proposes a new horizon for the theology of marriage.

I conclude that the answer to the fifth question is yes; John Paul's *Theology of the Body* proposal has consequences for theology as a whole. John Paul's theological anthropology is centered on his theological understanding of the conjugal act. He heralds the need for an adequate theological anthropology; he characterizes the unity of *Theology of the Body* and *Humanae Vitae* as organic and homogeneous; and he explains that the questions to which the *Theology of the Body* responds spring from *Humanae Vitae*. The primary objective of the entire *Theology of the Body* is to meet the need to secure, reinforce and deepen *Humanae Vitae's* foundational theological anthropology.

However, theological anthropology is foundational to theology as a whole, and developments in theological anthropology necessarily ripple through all theology. This rippling effect comes into view when we consider that the *Theology of the Body's* understanding of the sacramental signification of the conjugal act includes the entire sacramental order, the order of grace, and the mysteries of the Blessed Trinity, Creation, Redemption and Sanctification.

I conclude that the sixth question, whether the development of *Humanae Vitae* proposed by the *Theology of the Body* portends genuine developments of Christian doctrine above and beyond *Humanae Vitae*, cannot be answered within the scope of this research. Much work remains for theologians to pursue the theological horizons opened by John Paul's *Theology of the Body*. A lot of history remains to unfold before John Paul's proposal may gain recognition as established Church doctrine and we do not know how its consequences may present themselves as future developments for theology as a whole.

On the other hand, we do know that the historical circumstance of new contraceptive technologies, and demographic and economic fears, challenged Church teaching on the morality of contraception. We know that *Humanae Vitae* addressed the problem but did not fully achieve its pastoral objective. We know that John Paul's *Theology of the Body* responded to Paul VI's call to deepen the theological understanding of conjugal love. We know that as a theological development the *Theology of the Body* eschewed the tired polemics of moral theology, casuistry, natural law and the metaphysics of being, and focused instead on the subjective and anagogic rather than the objective and tropological dimensions of the conjugal act. We know that John Paul's exegeses of the mystical sense and intelligence of Scripture, discovered the conjugal act to be a theological wellspring from which flows the sacramental signification of Christian mysteries, sacraments and grace. We also know that John Paul's proposal survives scrutiny by Saint John Henry Newman's very well architected tests designed to expose doctrinal proposals that are corruptions or innovations.

Many questions remain: whether the *Theology of the Body* is an adequate response to Paul VI's call for a deeper theological understanding of conjugal love; and whether, as a Church teaching, the *Theology of the Body* is an efficacious remedy to the deconstruction of marriage and family occasioned in large part by the pastoral failure of *Humanae Vitae*. While much further study may be warranted, I am persuaded the answer to both questions is yes.

As George Hayward Joyce, S.J. states in his historical and doctrinal study of Christian marriage: "The civilization of Christendom—the civilization of which we are the heirs—was founded on Christian Marriage."[230] If Joyce is correct, something very much like John Paul's monumental theological understanding of the conjugal act would seem commensurate with the challenges we face and be an adequate response to Paul VI's call for a deeper theological understanding of conjugal love. The Church is in extreme need of an efficacious response to the increasingly dissolute and barren Christendom born of the pastoral failure of *Humanae Vitae*.

---

[230] George Hayward Joyce, S.J., *Christian Marriage: An Historical and Doctrinal Study*, *Heythorp Series: I* (London: Sheed & Ward, 1933).

Moreover, as we swelter in the rising temperature of the newest monumental clergy sex and money scandals, there is a primary nexus that is easy to miss, -that deconstruction of the clergy proceeds from deconstruction of marriage and the family. If we fail to grasp that nexus, we will continue to ruminate in a hunt for secondary causes and solutions, and continue to fail. So the question is: can the Church come to grips with the deconstruction of marriage and family? My answer is yes; she can enjoy a favorable sea change and an incoming tide uplifting all boats, as she grows into Pope Saint John Paul's theological anthropology, -as her doctrine.

✝

REFERENCES

PRIMARY SOURCES - SCRIPTURE

Revised Standard Version Bible, Ignatius Edition. Second Catholic Edition ed. San Francisco: Thomas Nelson Publishing, for Ignatius Press, 2006.

PRIMARY SOURCES - MAGISTERIAL DOCUMENTS

"Session 5." *Ecumenical Council IV* (451). http://www.newadvent.org/fathers/3811.htm.

Catechism of the Catholic Church, 2016. Accessed May 2016. http://www.vatican.va/archive/ENG0015/ INDEX.HTM.

John Paul II, Pope. "Catechesis in Our Time." (1979): 67. Accessed 10/16/1979. http://w2.vatican.va/content/john-paul-ii/en/apost exhortations/documents/hf jp-ii exh 16101979 catechesi-tradendae.html.

John Paul II, Pope. "Familiaris Consortio." (Nov. 22, 1981 1981). Accessed 2018. http://w2.vatican.va/content/john-paul-ii/en/apost exhortations/documents/hf jp-ii exh 19811122 familiaris-consortio.html.

John Paul II, Pope. *The Theology of the Body: Human Love in the Divine Plan*. Boston: Daughters of Saint Paul, 1997.

John Paul II, Pope. *Fides Et Ratio: Encyclical on Faith and Reason*, 1999. http://w2.vatican.va/content/john-paul-ii/en/encyclicals/documents/hf_jp-ii_enc_14091998_fides-et-ratio.html.

John Paul II, Pope. *The Role of the Christian Family in the Modern World*. Boston: Daughters of Saint Paul, 1999.

John Paul II, Pope. *Man and Woman He Created Them; a Theology of the Body*. Translated by Michael Waldstein. Boston: Pauline Books & Media, 2006

Paul VI, Pope. "Gaudium Et Spes; the Pastoral Constitution on the Church in the Modern World." (1965). Accessed 2018. http://www.vatican.va/archive/hist_councils/ii_vatican_council/documents/vat-ii_const_19651207_gaudium-et-spes_en.html.

Paul VI, Pope. "Humanae Vitae " Vatican Press. Last modified July 25 1968. Accessed 2016. http://w2.vatican.va/content/paul-vi/en/encyclicals/documents/hf_p-vi_enc_25071968_humanae-vitae.html

Vatican Council, II *Gaudium Et Spes; Pastoral Constitution on the Church in the Modern World*. Vol. 1. The Vatican Collection; Vatican Council 2, Conciliar and Post Conciliar Documents, edited by Austin Flannery O.P. Northport N.Y. : Dominican Publications, 1965.

PRIMARY SOURCES - CHURCH FATHERS AND DOCTORS

Anselm, St., Archbishop of Canterbury. *Why God Became Man and the Virgin Conception and Original Sin.* Translated by Joseph M. Colleran. Albany: Image Books, 1969.

Aquinas, Thomas Saint. *Summa Theologica.* Translated by Fathers of the English Dominican Province. Vol. I. 2nd ed. London: Burns Oates & Washbourne Ltd., 1922.

Aquinas, Thomas Saint. *Summa Theologica.* Translated by Fathers of the English Dominican Provence. Vol. 1, 5 vols. Complete English Edition ed. Westminster, MD: Christian Classics 1981.

Augustine, Saint. *The Trinity.* Translated by Stephen McKenna CSSR. The Fathers of the Church. Washington DC: Catholic University of America Press, 1963.

Augustine, Saint. *Augustine on Marriage and Sexuality.* Washington DC: Catholic University of America Press, 1996.

Augustine, Saint. *On Genesis: A Refutation of the Manichees.* Hyde Park, NY: New City Press, 2002.

Augustine, Saint. *Augustine in His Own Words.* edited by William Harmless S.J. Washington, DC: The Catholic University of America, 2010.

Augustine, Saint. "Sermon # 2." *Nicene and Post-Nicene Fathers, First Series, Vol. 6.* (1888). Accessed 9/21/2017. http://www.newadvent.org/fathers/160302.htm.

Bonaventure. *Breviloquium*. Translated by Erwin Esser Nemmers. St. Louis: B. Herder Book Co., 1946.

Chrysostom, John. *On Marriage and Family Life*. Translated by Catherine P. Roth & David Anderson. Popular Patristic Series, edited by John Behr. Crestwood, NY: St. Vladimir's Seminary Press, 2003.

Nyssa, Gregory of. "On the Making of Man." (2005). http://www.ccel. org/ccel/schaff/npnf205.pdf.

Origen. *Origen on First Principles* [De Principiis]. Translated by G. W. Butterworth. Gloucester: Peter Smith 1973.

Origen. *Homilies on Genesis and Exodus*. The Fathers of the Church: A New Translation, edited by Hermigild Dressler O.F.M. et. al.: Catholic University of America Press, 1982.

Origen. *Dialogue of Origen with Heraclides and His Fellow Bishops on the Father the Son and the Soul*. Translated by Robert J. Daly S.J. Ancient Christian Writers, edited by Walter J. Burghardt et. al. New York: Paulist Press, 1992.

PRIMARY SOURCES - WORKS OF KAROL WOJTYLA

John Paul II, Pope. "Letter to Families." (1994): 76. Accessed 2001. https://www.ewtn.com/library/papaldoc/jp2famlt.htm.

John Paul II, Pope. "Magnum Matrimonii Sacramentum; Apostolic Constitution." (2007). https://www.catholicculture.org/culture/library/view.cfm?recnum=6408.

Wojtyla, Karol. "Subjectivity and the Irreducible in the Human Being." In *Catholic Thought from Lublin: Person and Community*, edited by Andrew N. Woznicki. New York: Peter Lang, 1993.

Wojtyla, Karol *Love and Responsibility*. Translated by H. T. Willetts. San Francisco: Ignatius Press, 1960.

Wojtyla, Karol *Person and Community: Selected Essays*. Translated by Theresa Sandok OSM. Vol. 4. Catholic Thought from Lublin, edited by Andrew N. Woznicki. NY: Peter Lang, 1993.

PRIMARY SOURCES - WORKS OF JOHN HENRY NEWMAN

Newman, John Henry. *An Essay on the Development of Christian Doctrine*. Notre Dame Series in the Great Books. Notre Dame IN: University of Notre Dame Press, 1878.

Newman, John Henry. *Letters and Correspondence of John Henry Newman*. Vol. 2, edited by Anne Mozley. London: Longmans, Green and Co., 1890.

Newman, John Henry. *An Essay in Aid of a Grammar of Assent: Introduction by Etienne Gilson*. Garden City NY: Image Books, 1955.

Newman, John Henry. *Apologia Pro Vita Sua*. Garden City: Image Books, 1956.

Newman, John Henry. *The Heart of Newman: Synthesis Arr. By Erich Przywara, S.J.;Introduction by Msgr. H. Francis Davis*. Springfield, IL: Templegate, 1963.

Newman, John Henry. *The Philosophical Notebook of John Henry Newman.* Vol. II, edited by Edward Sillem. Louvain, Belgium: Nauwelaerts Publishing House, 1970.

Newman, John Henry. *An Essay in Aid of a Grammar of Assent: Introduction by Nicholas Lash.* Notra Dame, IN: University of Notre Dame Press, 1979.

Newman, John Henry. *A Packet of Letters.* Edited by Joyce Sugg. New York: Oxford University Press, 1983.

Newman, John Henry. *Roman Catholic Writings on Doctrinal Development.* Edited and translated by James Gaffney. Kansas City: Sheed & Ward, 1997.

Newman, John Henry. *An Essay on the Development of Christian Doctrine [1845].* Edited by Stanley L. Jaki. Pinckney, Michigan: Real View Books, 2003.

Newman, John Henry. *Fifteen Sermons, Preached before the University of Oxford.* 3rd ed. Notre Dame Series in the Great Books. South Bend: University of Notre Dame Press, 2003.

Newman, John Henry. "The Theory of Developments in Religious Doctrine." In *Fifteen Sermons Preached before the University of Oxford,* 351. South Bend: University of Notre Dame Press, 2003.

SECONDARY SOURCES - BOOKS

Wing to Wing, Oar to Oar: Readings on Courting and Marrying. Edited by Amy Kass & Leon Kass. The Ethics of Everydy Life. Indiana: University of Notre Dame Press, 2000.

Aquinas on Doctrine: A Critical Introduction. Edited by Thomas G. Weinandy O.F.M. Cap. Daniel A Keating & John P. Yocum. London: T&T Clark, 2004.

The Theology of Thomas Aquinas. edited by Rik Van Nieuwenhove & Joseph Wawrykow. Notre Dame, Indiana: University of Notre Dame Press, 2005.

2000, Theological-Historical Commission for the Great Jubilee of the Year. *The Eucharist: Gift of Divine Life.* Translated by Robert R. Barr. New York: Crossroad Publishing Company, 1999.

Stanley Jaki. *Newman's Challenge.* Grand Rapids: William B. Eerdmans, 2000.

Adler, Mortimer J. *Ten Philosophical Mistakes.* NY: Macmillan, 1985.

Allen, Sister Prudence, R.S.M. *The Concept of Woman: The Aristotelian Revolution, 750b.C. - A.D. 1250.* Grand Rapids MI: William B. Eerdmans, 1985.

Asci, Donald P. *The Conjugal Act as a Personal Act.* San Francisco: Ignatius, 2002.

Balthasar, Hans Urs Von *Cosmic Liturgy: The Universe According to Maximus the Confessor.* Translated by Brian E. Daley S.J. San Francisco: Ignatius Press, 2003.

Balthasar, Hans Urs Von *The Von Balthasar Reader.* Edited by Medard Kehl S.J. and Werner Loser S.J. Translated by Robert J. Daly S.J. and Fred Lawrence. New York: Crossroads, 1982.

Balthasar, Hans Urs Von *Origen Spirit and Fire: A Thematic Anthology of His Writings*. Translated by Robert J. Daly S.J. Washington, D.C.: The Catholic University of America Press, 1984.

Behr, John. *Asceticism and Anthropology in Irenaeus and Clement*. Oxford: Oxford University Press, 2000.

Bingen, Hildegard of. *Scivias*. Translated by Colomba Hart & Jane Bishop. Classics of Western Spirituality, edited by Bernard McGinn. Mahwah, NJ: Paulist Press, 1990.

Brown, Peter. *The Body and Society: Men, Women and Sexual Renunciation in Early Christianity*. American Lectures on the History of Religions, edited by Committee on the History of Religions of the American Council of Learned Societies. New York: Columbia University Press, 1988.

Buchanan, Patrick J. *Death of the West: How Populations and Immigrant Invasions Imperil Our Country and Civilization*. New York: Thomas Dunne Books, 2002.

Buckley, Michael S.J. *At the Origins of Modern Athiesm*. New Haven: Yale University Press, 1987.

Burns, J. Patout. *Theological Anthropology*. Translated by J. Patout Burns. Sources of Early Christian Thought, edited by William Rusch. Philadelphia: Fortress Press, 1981.

Buttiglione, Rocco. *Karol Wojtyla: The Thought of the Man Who Became Pope John Paul 2nd*. Grand Rapids MI: William B. Eerdmans, 1997.

Crosby, John F. *The Personalism of John Henry Newman*. Washington DC: Catholic University of America Press, 2014.

de Lubac, Henri Cardinal S.J. *The Splendor of the Church*. Translated by Michael Mason. New York: Sheed and Ward, 1956.

Gendron, Lionel. *Mystery of the Trinity and Familial Symbolism: An Historical Approach*. Rome: Pontifica Universitas Gregoriana, 1975.

Hobbel, Arne J. "The Imago Dei in the Writings of Origen." *Studia Patristica* 21 (1989).

Irigaray, Luce. *An Ethics of Sexual Difference*. Translated by Carolyn Burke & Gillian C. Gill. Ithica, NY: Cornell University Press, 1993. Originally published as Ethique de la difference sexuelle.

J. M. Waliggo, A. Roest Crollius S.J., T. Nkeramihigo S.J., J. Mutiso-MBinda. *Inculturation; Its Meaning and Urgency*. Kampala: Saint Paul Publications-Africa/Daughters of St. Paul, 1986.

Jeffery, Peter CSSP. *The Mystery of Christian Marriage*. Mahwah, NJ: Paulist Press, 2006.

Joyce, George Hayward S.J. *Christian Marriage: An Historical and Doctrinal Study*. Heythorp Series: I. London: Sheed & Ward, 1933.

Judaeus, Philo. *The Essential Philo*. edited by Nahum N. Glatzer. New York: Schocken Books, 1971.

Kasper, Walter. *Theology and Church*. Translated by Margret Kohl. New York: Crossroads, 1989.

Keefe, Donald J., S.J. *Covenental Theology*. Novato CA: Presidio Press, 1996.

Kelly, Joseph F. *The Ecumenical Councils of the Catholic Church: A History.* Collegeville, MN: The Liturgical Press: A Michael Glazier Book, 2009.

Ker, Ian. *John Henry Newman; a Biography.* Vol. II. Oxford: Oxford University Press, 1990.

Kerr, Fergus. *Twentieth Century Catholic Theologians.* Oxford: Blackwell publishing, 2007.

Kerr, Fergus. *Thomas Aquinas: A Very Short Introduction.* Oxford: Oxford University Press, 2009.

King, Christopher J. *Origen on the Song of Songs as the Spirit of Scripture: The Bridegroom's Perfect Marriage-Song.* Oxford Theological Monographs, edited by J. Day et.al. New York: Oxford University Press Inc., 2005.

LeMasters, Philip Ph.D. *Toward a Eucharistic Vision of Church, Family, Marriage & Sex.* Minneapolis, MN: Light and Life Publishing, 2004.

Levering, Matthew. *Scripture and Metaphysics: Aquinas and the Renewal of Trinitarian Theology.* Challenges in Contemporary Theology, edited by Gareth Jones and Lewis Ayers. Oxford: Blackwell Publishing Ltd., 2004.

Leyerle, Blake. *Theatrical Shows and Ascetic Lives: John Chrysostom's Attack on Spiritual Marriage.* Berkley: University of California Press, 2001.

Louth, Andrew. *Maximus the Confessor.* The Early Church Fathers, edited by Carol Harrison. London: Routledge, 1966.

MacIntyre, Alasdair. *Whose Justice? Which Rationality?* Notre Dame, Indiana: University of Notre Dame Press, 1988. Reprint, 4th.

MacIntyre, Alasdair. *Three Rival Versions of Moral Enquiry: Encyclopedia, Genealogy, and Tradition*. Notre Dame, IN: University of Notre Dame Press, 1990.

Mackin, Theodore S.J. *What Is Marriage*. New York: Paulist Press, 1982.

Marcel, Gabriel. *The Mystery of Being: Reflections & Mystery*. Translated by G.S. Frasier. Vol. I, II vols. Chicago IL: Henry Regnery Company, 1950.

Marcel, Gabriel. *The Mystery of Being: Faith and Reality*. Translated by Rene Hague. Vol. II, II vols. London: The Harvill Press Ltd., 1951.

Marcel, Gabriel. *The Philosophy of Existentialism*. New York: The Citadel Press, 2002.

Maritain, Jacques. *A Preface to Metaphysics: Seven Lectures on Being*. New York: Sheed & Ward, 1948.

Meyendorff, John. *Marriage: An Orthodox Perspective*. Tuckahoe, N.Y.: St. Vladimir's Seminary Press, 1970.

Miller, Paula Jean. *Marriage: The Sacrament of Divine-Human Communion*. Vol. One: A Commentary on St. Bonaventure's Breviloquium. Quincy, IL: Franciscan Press, 1996.

Nellas, Panayiotis. *Deification in Christ: Orthodox Perspectives on the Nature of the Human Person*. Translated by Norman Russell. Contemporary Greek Theologians, edited by Christos Yannaras. Crestwood NY: St. Vladimir's Seminary Press, 1987.

Norris, Richard A Jr. *The Christological Controversy*. Translated by Richard A. Norris Jr. Sources of Early Christian Thought, edited by William G. Rusch. Philadelphia: Fortress Press, 1980.

Ouellet, Marc Cardinal. *Divine Likeness: Toward a Trinitarian Anthropologgy of the Family*. Translated by Philip Milligan and Linda M. Cicone. Ressourcement. Grand Rapids: William B. Eerdmans, 2006.

Percy, Anthony. *Theology of the Body Made Simple*. Boston MA: Pauline Books and Media, 2005.

Pinckaers, Servais O.P., ed. *The Sources of Christian Ethics*. Translated by Sister Mary Thomas Noble O.P. Washington DC: Catholic University of America Press, 1995.

Pinckaers, Servais O.P. *Morality: The Catholic View*. Translated by Michael Sherwin O.P. South Bend, Indiana: St. Augustine's Press, 2003. Originally published as La Morale Catholique.

Plato. *Timaeus, Critias, Cleitophon, Menexenus, and Epistles*. Loeb Classic Library, edited by R.G. Bury. London: William Heinemann 1929.

Prokes, Sister Mary Timothy, FSE. *Toward a Theology of the Body*. Grand Rapids: William B.Eerdmans, 1996.

Quay, Paul M. S.J. *The Christian Meaning of Human Sexuality*. Evanston: Credo House, 1985.

Rahner, Karl S.J. "The Word in History." In *The St. Xavier Symposium*, edited by T. Patrick Burke, 23. New York: Sheed and Ward, 1996.

Rahner, Karl, S.J. *The Trinity.* Translated by Joseph Donceel. New York: The Crossroads Publishing Company, 1997.

Ratzinger, Joseeph. *The Nature and Mission of Theology: Approaches to Understanding Its Role in the Light of Present Controversy.* Translated by Adrian Walker. San Francisco: Ignatius Press, 1995.

Ricoeur, Paul. *Biblical Hermeneutics* edited by John Dominic Crossan:. Missoula Montana: University of Montana, 1975.

Rist, John M. *Platonism and Its Chrstian Heritage.* London: Valorum Reprints, 1985.

Rist, John M. *Augustine: Ancient Thought Baptized.* Cambridge: Cambridge University Press, 1994.

Rowland, Tracy. *Culture and the Thomist Tradition; after Vatican 2.* Radical Orthodoxy, edited by Cathrine Pickstock and Graham Ward John Milbank. London: Routledge, 2003.

Royal, Robert. *A Deeper Vision: The Catholic Intellectual Tradition in the Twentieth Century.* San Francisco: Ignatius, 2015.

Scheeben, Matthias Joseph. *The Mysteries of Christianity.* Translated by Cyril Vollert S.J. New York: A Herder & Herder Book, Crossroads Publishing Company, 1946.

Schindler, D. C. *The Catholicity of Reason.* Ressourcement: Retrieval and Renewal in Catholic Thought, edited by David L. Schindler. Grand Rapids MI: Wm. B. Eerdmans, 2013.

Schmitz, Kenneth L. *At the Center of the Human Drama: The Philosophical Anthropology of Karol Wojtyla / John Paul 2.* Washington DC: Catholic University of America Press, 1993.

Schmitz, Kenneth L. . *The Gift: Creation.* The Aquinas Lecture. Milwaukee: Marquette University Press, 1982.

Scola, Angelo. *The Nuptial Mystery.* Translated by Michelle K. Borras. Ressourcement, edited by David L. Schindler. Grand Rapids, Michigan /Cambridge U.K.: English Translation, William B. Eerdmans Publishing Company, 2005. Originally published as Il mistero nuzaile. 1. Uomo-donna --- 2. Matrimonio-Famiglia by Paul-Mursia, Rome, 1998-2000.

Shivanandan, Mary. *Crossing the Threshold of Love:A New Vision of Marriage in Light of John Paul 2nd's Anthropology"* Washington DC: Catholic University of America Press, 2002.

Shults, F. LeRon. *Reforming Theological Anthropology: After the Philosophical Turn to Relationality.* Grand Rapids, MI: Wm. B. Eerdmans, 2003.

Sokolowski, Robert. *The God of Faith and Reason: Foundations of Christian Theology.* 2nd ed. Washington, D.C.: Catholic University of America Press, 1995.

Spaemann, Robert. *Love & the Dignity of Human Life: On Nature and Natural Law.* Grand Rapids, MI: Wm. B. Eerdmans, 2012.

St. Victor, Richard of *On the Trinity.* Translated by Ruben Angelici. Eugene, OR: Cascade Books, 2011.

Thunberg, Lars. *Man and the Cosmos: The Vision of Saint Maximus the Confessor.* Crestwood NY: St. Vladimir's Seminary Press, 1985.

Tollefsen, Torstein Theodor. *The Christocentric Cosmology of St Maximus the Confessor*. The Oxford Early Christian Studies Series, edited by Gillian Clark and Andrew Louth. New York: Oxford University Press, 2008.

Wahba, Mathias F. *Honorable Marriage According to Saint Athanasius*. Minneapolis MN: Light and Life Publishing, 1996.

Weigel, George. *The Truth of Catholicism: Ten Controversies Explored*. New York: Harper Collins, 2001.

Weigel, George. *Witness to Hope*. Baltimore: Cliff Street Books, 2001.

Weigel, George. *The Courage to Be Catholic: Crisis, Reform and the Future of the Church*. New York: Basic Books, 2002.

Weinandy, Thomas G., O.F.M. Cap. *The Father's Spirit of Sonship: Reconceiving the Trinity*. Edinburgh: T&T Clark, 1993.

Weinandy, Thomas G., O.F.M. Cap. *Does God Suffer?* Notre Dame: University of Notre Dame Press, under licence from Lic. T&T Clark Ltd., Edinburgh, 2000.

Weinandy, Thomas G., O.F.M. Cap. *Essays in Christology*. Faith & Reason: Studies in Catholic Theology and Philosophy. Ave Maria, Florida: Sapientia Press, 2014.

West, Christopher. *The Theology of the Body Explained: A Commentary on John Paul 2nd's "Gospel of the Body"*. Boston: Pauline Books and Media, 2003.

West, Christopher. *Theology of the Body for Beginners: A Basic Introduction to John Paul 2ⁿᵈ's Sexual Revolution*. West Chester, NJ: Ascension Press, 2004.

Wilken, Robert Louis. *The Spirit of Early Christian Thought*. New Haven CT: Yale University Press, 2003.

Young, Frances M. *From Nicaea to Chalcedon: A Guide to the Literature and Its Background*. Second ed. Grand Rapids Michigan: Baker Academic, a division of Baker Publishing Group, 2010.

Zizioulas, John D. *Being as Communion*. Crestwood, NY: St. Vladimir's Press, 1985.

Zizioulas, John D. *Communion and Otherness: Further Studies in Personhood and the Church*. edited by Paul McPartlan. London: T&T Clark, 2006.

SECONDARY SOURCES - BOOK CHAPTERS

Bonino, Serge-Thomas O.P. "An Introduction to the Document *in Search of a Universal Ethic: A New Look at the Natural Law*." In *Searching for a Universal Ethic: Multidisciplinary, Ecumenical, and Interfaith Responses to the Catholic Natural Law Tradition*, edited by John Berkman and William C. Mattison III. Grand Rapida: William B. Eerdmans, 2014.

Clarke, Norris W., S.J. . "The Integration of Personalism and Thomistic Metaphysics in 21ˢᵗ Century Thomism." In *The Creative Retrieval of Saint Thomas Aquinas: Essays in Thomistic Philosophy, New and Old*, 11. New York: Fordham University Press 2009.

Crollius, Ary Roest, S.J. "Inculturation: Newness and Ongoing Process." 12. Kampala: St. Paul Publications-Africa/Daughters of St. Paul, 1986.

Crollius, Ary Roest S.J. "The Meaning of Culture in Theological Anthropology." In *Inculturation: Its Meaning and Urgency*, 19. Kampala: St. Paul Publications-Africa/Daughters of St. Paul, 1986.

Ladner, Gerhart B. "The Philosophical Anthropology of Gregory of Nyssa." *Dumbarton Oaks Papers* 12 (1958).

Meilaender, Gilbert. "Can't We All Just Get Along?" In *Searching for a Universal Ethic: Multidisciplinary, Ecumenical, and Interfaith Responses to the Catholic Natural Law Tradition*, edited by John Berkman and William C. Mattison III. Grand Rapids: William B. Eerdmans, 2014.

Melina, Livio. "Pragmatic and Christological Foundations of Natural Law." In *Searching for a Universal Ethic: Multidisciplinary, Ecumenical, and Interfaith Responses to the Catholic Natural Law Tradition*, edited by John Berkman and William C. Mattison III. Grand Rapids: William B Eerdmans, 2014.

Milbank, John. "Henri De Lubac." In *The Modern Theologians: An Introduction to Christian Theology since 1918*, edited by David F. Ford with Rachel Muers, 76-91. Malden MA: Blackwell, 2005.

Mutiso-Mbinda, John "Inculturation: Challenge to the African Local Church." In *Inculturation: Its Meaning and Its Urgency*, 9. Kampala: St. Paul Publications-Africa/Daughters of St. Paul, 1886.

Nkeramihigo, Theoneste S.J. "Introduction: Inculturation of Christianity." In *Inculturation*, 8. Kampala: St. Paul Publications-Africa/Daughters of St. Paul, 1986.

Waliggo, John Mary. "Making a Church That Is Truly African." In *Inculturation; Its Meaning and Urgency*, 20. Kampala: St. Paul Publications-Africa/Daughters of St. Paul, 1986.

Woods, Thomas E. Jr. *How the Catholic Church Built Western Civilization.* Washington: Regnery Publishing, Inc., 2005.

SECONDARY SOURCES - ARTICLES

Baur, Chrysostom. "St. John Chrysostom: Chrysostom as Dogmatic Theologian." *The Catholic Encyclopedia* (1913). http://www.newadvent.org/cathen/08452b.htm.

Bavel O.S.A., Johannes. "The Anthropology of Augustine." *Études Augustiniennes* no. 19 (1973): 158-62.

Crosby, John F. "What We Mean by Personalism." (Accessed 2016. http://www.thepersonalistproject.org/about_us.

Ford, John T. C.S.C. "Two Recent Studies on Newman." *The Thomist* 41, no. 3 (July 1977).

Keefe, Donald J. S.J. *"Basar-Nepes: Sarx-Pneuma; Body-Soul: Death-Resurrection: An Essay on Pauline Anthropology"* ITEST. Saint Louis: FAITH/SCIENCE PRESS, 2000.

Purves, James G. M. . "The Spirit and the Imago Dei: Reviewing the Anthropology of Irenaeus of Lyons." *Paternoster Periodicals* LXVII, no. 2 (April 1996): 106.

Ratzinger, Joseph. "Retrieving the Tradition: Concerning the Notion of Person in Theology." *Communio: International Catholic Review*, no. 3 Fall (1990): 439-54.

Runia, D. T. "God and Man in Philo of Alexandria." *Journal of Theological Studies*, no. 39 (April 1988).

Various. *Catholic Encyclopedia Patristic Series*: New Advent, 1910. http://www.newadvent.org/cathen/08452b.htm

Various. *In Search of a Universal Ethic: A New Look at the Natural Law.* The Vatican International Theological Commission, 2009.

Various. *Sensus Fidei in the Life of the Church* Rome: International Theological Commission, 2014.

Weigel, George. "John Paul and the Crisis of Humanism." *First Things*, December 1999.

APPENDIX

Defense Questions and Answers:

1. Please identify the nature and scope of the "original contribution" your thesis has made to the subject which was not there before you conducted your research and wrote the thesis.

There is much that is original in the *Theology of the Body* and this dissertation. However, the principal original contribution of the dissertation is its argument that the subject matter and unifying theme of the *Theology of the Body* is a Christian understanding of the conjugal act which develops the doctrine of *Humanae Vitae*.

Much of the literature recognizes that the *Theology of the Body* celebrates sex, marriage and family as holy and conducive to salvation. Authors take pains to reconcile the gift-ethics of the *Theology of the Body* with the virtue-ethics of Thomas Aquinas. The mutual self-giving and receiving, and the formation of a communion of persons are recognized to be Trinitarian and Christological themes. Generally, these themes are treated as lofty analogical expressions of mystical devotion, spiritualism or sermonizing, not as sacramental and integral developments of the Catholic doctrinal tradition.

By contrast, the dissertation identifies the *Theology of the Body's* link to the doctrinal tradition in John Paul's conclusion: "In some sense, one can even say that all the reflections dealing with the 'Redemption of the

Body and the Sacramentality of Marriage' seem to constitute an extensive commentary on the doctrine contained precisely in *Humanae Vitae*." (TOB 133.2). *Humanae Vitae's* moral doctrine is that all conjugal acts must remain open to the transmission of life (HV 11).

Linking the *Theology of the Body* to the doctrinal tradition by way of *Humanae Vitae's* moral doctrine constitutes a compelling call for theologians to investigate the *Theology of the Body's* anthropological understanding of the conjugal act in a doctrinal perspective. John Paul explicitly pointed to the need to build an adequate theological anthropology (TOB 13.2). Paul VI, and the Synod of bishops that led to John Paul's encyclical *Familiaris Consortio*, respectively "emphasized the possibility of deepening the explanation of Christian truth in this area," and called upon theologians "to work out more completely the biblical and personalistic aspects of the doctrine contained in *Humanae Vitae*," (TOB 133.2). The original contribution of the dissertation, like the entire *Theology of the Body*, is in some way occupied with different dimensions of this imperative investigation. Methodologically, the dissertation remains scrupulously close to the text of the *Theology of the Body* and other writings of the sainted pope. Repeated, direct citations of his works ensure that its inferences are not thought to be those of the author but rather those of John Paul.

The gravity of the tasks set out for theologians (of building an adequate theological anthropology, of deepening the explanation of Christian truth in this area, and of working out more completely the biblical and personalistic aspects of the doctrine contained in *Humanae Vitae*) comes into view, when we realize that doctrinal developments affect the whole body of doctrine like ripples in a pond, yeast in a loaf, or a rising tide that raises all boats. Newman explains this effect in his third test of genuine doctrinal developments: the power of assimilation.

2. In what specific way(s) does your dissertation shed light on the understanding of the Christian mysteries of the Blessed Trinity, the sacramental order and the order of grace?

Specifically, the dissertation shows that John Paul's *Theology of the Body* sheds light upon our understanding of the Christian mysteries of the Blessed Trinity, creation, redemption and sanctification, as well as upon the sacramental order and the order of grace by virtue of its understanding of the sacramentality of marriage.

The *Theology of the Body* is a work of theological anthropology that, by definition, seeks to give an account of the mysteries of creation, redemption and sanctification. It is a scriptural exegesis searching revelation and sacred tradition for a deeper understanding of Christian mysteries. The *Theology of the Body's* first step is to focus on Christ's own exegetical interpretation of the old testament and the beginning (Gn. 1:27 and 2:24) in his discussion of divorce with the Pharisees (Mt. 19; Mk. 10). Christ's account insists that marriage is irrevocable or indissoluble because two become one flesh in the conjugal act.

John Paul's next step is to explain the dimension of gift in the mystery of creation. Creating Adam in His own image is a gift of Himself given by God to Adam. Creation of Eve is likewise a gift of Himself given by God to Eve. By the creation of Eve, the creation of man is completed. By the creation of Eve, the image of God in Man is also completed. Importantly, the Creation of Eve creates a potential for Adam and Eve to be mutual gifts to one another, and to be holy.

By God's command to increase, multiply and have dominion, God gives the world to man, and God gives man freedom, and particularly the freedom of the gift to realize the potential to be mutual gifts to one another. In this way the mystery of creation is understood in the dimension of gift. It is noteworthy that according to the *Theology of the Body* holiness entered the world with the creation of Eve (TOB 19.5).

In the dimension of the gift, man is understood to be in the image of God typologically. The free mutual giving and receiving of the Father and the Son and free procession of the Holy Spirit therefrom, are the prototype of the free mutual giving and receiving of Adam and Eve and the free procession of progeny therefrom. In this way the *Theology of the Body* sheds light on our understanding of the sacramentality of marriage as a sign, image and type, of its prototype, which is the Communion of Persons of the immanent Blessed Trinity (TOB 9.5).

Saint Paul's teaching on marriage (Eph. 5:21-33,) is another major focus of the *Theology of the Body*. Likening marriage to the self-gift of Christ to the Church together with the Church's reciprocal devotion to Christ is a second prototype of which the conjugal act is a type. Here it is a sacramental sign of the Blessed Trinity in its economic activity, the drama and mystery of redemption.

The *Theology of the Body* understands the mystery of sanctification in like manner. Creation and redemption are understood as self-gifts by God to man: the self-gift of His image in creation; and, the self-gift of His life in redemption. This establishes that God's gifts are gifts of Himself limited only by man's capacity for reception of God's self-gift. The Christian understanding of eschatological sanctification is that in the sanctified state, man's capacity to receive God's self-gift is enhanced to a degree we do not yet comprehend. This is how the conjugal act is also a sign and sacrament of the mystery of sanctification and how *Theology of the Body* sheds light on the mystery of sanctification.

The unifying thread running through Trinitarian and Christological theology and the mysteries of creation, redemption and sanctification is God's self-gift to man of which the mutual self-gift of the conjugal act is a sacrament. The sacramental order is the providential means of accessing God's self-gift in this life. The order of grace is the order of God's giving of Himself to man: as His image in the mystery of creation, in the sacramental order in this life through the mystery of redemption, and in the mystery of sanctification in life to come.

By virtue of creation in His image, the mutual irrevocable self-gift of man and wife in marriage and its conjugal embrace is a sacramental sign of the immanent life of the Blessed Trinity. It is a sacramental sign of the economic Blessed Trinity by God's action in our redemption, and it is a sacramental sign of God's self-gift to the sanctified in the eschaton. In these specific ways, according to the *Theology of the Body*, conjugal love, expressed in the conjugal act, is a sacramental sign of the Blessed Trinity, of creation, redemption and sanctification, from which it follows that the conjugal act, as a matter of theological anthropology is the foundation of the sacramental order and the order of grace.

3. Could you substantiate your argument that Pope John Paul II's catechesis on the *Theology of the Body* represents a development of doctrine from Pope Paul VI's *Humanae Vitae* regarding the conjugal act?

I would substantiate my argument by offering reasons for my confidence. First, John Paul connected the entire *Theology of the Body* to Church doctrine by stating that: "In some sense, one can even say that all the reflections dealing with the 'Redemption of the Body and the Sacramentality of Marriage' seem to constitute an extensive commentary on the doctrine contained precisely in *Humanae Vitae*," (TOB 133.2). The doctrine contained precisely in *Humanae Vitae* is that every marital act must be open to the transmission of life, (HV 11). This explicit connection makes a serious inquiry into whether and how the *Theology of the Body* develops the doctrine of *Humanae Vitae* a theological imperative.

Second, John Paul also stated that the *Theology of the Body* is a catechesis (TOB 133.1), and, hence, a papal teaching on the anthropology of man as the image of God, and on the moral doctrine of *Humanae Vitae*. This gives me confidence that the dissertation is a worthwhile inquiry and fitting hermeneutic for a correct reading and understanding of the whole *Theology of the Body*.

Third, the dissertation compares both teachings to identify what is common to both and what the *Theology of the Body* adds that may develop *Humanae Vitae*. This analysis discovers that the conjugal act is the focus of both teachings, is presented differently in both teachings, and that the *Theology of the Body's* presentation constitutes a substantial enlargement of *Humanae Vitae's* anthropological understanding of the conjugal act.

Fourth, the entire dissertation, like the entire *Theology of the Body*, is occupied with different dimensions of this comparative analysis. Part I takes up different dimensions of this analysis in five chapters: Patristic and medieval theological anthropologies; natural law theory; personalism; ontology; and, the teaching authority of the ordinary magisterium. Part I surveys historical, philosophical and ecclesiological considerations all of which bear on the comparison. They each open an entry door to a fresh consideration of the subjects at hand; theological anthropology, marriage and the conjugal act.

Fifth, Part II formally compares both teachings as different literary genres and disparate theological treatises and Part III presents the *Theology of the Body's* enlargement of *Humanae Vitae's* anthropological understanding of the conjugal act. Part IV presents doctrinal development and Saint John Henry Newman's seven tests for genuine doctrinal developments and applies Newman's tests to John Paul's proposed development.

Sixth, in addition to the forgoing detailed procedural roadmap I am confident because of what the dissertation accomplishes. It shows that in the history of theological anthropology, the significance of God's creation of man in His image, as male and female, persists as an open question in every period of Church history. It illustrates contemporary debates between natural law theory and personalist theory. It recognizes competing ontologies (of being, consciousness, utility and relationality), and competing epistemologies (idealism, realism, materialism, utilitarianism). It describes the authorities of the magisterium in encyclicals and papal catecheses. It compares the Paul VI's encyclical and John Paul II's catechesis in the perspective of these considerations and criteria. It shows that in spite of their many differences, both teachings are compatible, complimentary, and in continuity, as each presents a different dimension of the theological anthropology of the conjugal act. These factors strengthen my confidence in the dissertation's argument.

These are my reasons for confidence that the dissertation substantiates the argument that the *Theology of the Body* develops *Humanae Vitae's* theological anthropology of the conjugal act. It enlarges *Humanae Vitae's* understanding and increases *Humanae Vitae's* intelligibility. Moreover, the dissertation shows that, according to the *Theology of the Body's* theological anthropology, the sacramental significance of the conjugal act is superabundant to the extent that it is identified with: the foundation of the sacramental order and the order of grace; a sacramental sign of the Blessed Trinity; Paul's *Magnum Mysterium* (Eph. 5, 21-31); and the great mystery hidden in God from eternity (Eph. 3:9).

Formal recognition as doctrine must wait for history: first, history has to crystallize the needs it addresses; and then, history has to issue its verdict with the support of the sense of the faithful.

There are abundant examples of theological anthropologies analogically relating the Blessed Trinity to the nuclear family in the history of Christianity. John Paul's genius was to reduce the nuclear family analogy down to its nuclear activity of the conjugal act itself, and then to unfold its sacramental signification to develop the moral doctrine that proscribes its desecration.

Despite high confidence in its argument, the dissertation does not assert that the *Theology of the Body's* inferences are doctrinal developments. Instead, it shows, as a minimum, that its inferences would not be disqualified on the basis of Newman's seven tests of genuine doctrinal developments.

4. As intended by John Paul II, the Theology of the Body should be understood as completely related to the doctrine of *Humanae Vitae*. How specifically does the structure and method of the Theology of the Body synchronize with those of *Humanae Vitae*?

As found in the title of my dissertation the common pivotal point at which both teachings meet is the conjugal act. Otherwise, as different genres, the two teachings differ in almost every respect and need synchronization. They have different goals, they frame their questions differently, they employ different ethical theories, ontologies, anthropologies, epistemologies, methodologies and authorities. This is addressed in detail in Part II of the dissertation. For example, *Humanae Vitae's* goal is to apply established Church teaching of moral doctrine to new circumstances, and the *Theology of the Body's* goal is to deepen the explanation of Christian truth, specifically, the Church's theological understanding of conjugal love and the conjugal act.

The first goal is to resolve a moral problem and the second goal is to improve an anthropological understanding. The dissertation introduced many of these disparate elements in the five chapters of Part I: chapter one samples anthropologies proposed by patristic and medieval theologians to illustrate their variety and the historical persistence of the anthropological question; chapter two presents strengths and weaknesses of contemporary deontological natural law theory; chapter three presents personalism as a rival of natural law in ethical theorizing; chapter four presents competing ontologies; and, chapter five discusses the authority of the ordinary magisterium.

All these chapters raise questions to prepare the ground for the comparative analysis of the two teaching documents. As Part II concludes, however, all the antinomies that make *Humanae Vitae* and the *Theology of the Body* different genres do not in any way nullify their theological unity, compatibility, complementarity and continuity nor diminish in any way the synchronization of the moral theological imperative of *Humanae Vitae* and the anthropological anagogic inferences of the *Theology of the Body*.

Both teachings are exegeses of scripture. However, *Humanae Vitae* interprets scripture in its moral or tropological sense whereas the *Theology of the Body* interprets scripture in its anagogic sense, meaning its ultimate spiritual or mystical sense. So, the *Theology of the Body* contains analysis after analysis of the meaning of creation of man as male and female in the image of God, and God's command to increase and multiply and have dominion over all creation. The *Theology of the Body* scrutinizes these Genesis scenes for their anagogic sense. Creating or giving man existence as male and female, in the image of God, giving man freedom, giving man dominion and giving man the command to increase and multiply, are all analyzed as fundamental to a theological understanding of the conjugal act. Accordingly, by obeying God's first command, man gives homage to God, praises God and worships God. This is an example of the anagogic sense of Scripture.

John Paul points out early on in the *Theology of the Body* that theology is always mediated by philosophy which is a conceptual language *par excellence* (TOB 3.3 footnote #6). Philosophically speaking, the *Theology of the Body* mediates the anagogic sense using different philosophical tools from those *Humanae Vitae* uses to mediate Scripture's moral sense. The *Theology of the Body* favors: phenomenology and induction over deontology and deduction; typology over predication; an ontology of person over an ontology of being; and, it favors an epistemology of subjective experience over an epistemology of objective logical necessity. These differences allow the *Theology of the Body* and *Humanae Vitae* to reach valid theological conclusions by travelling different philosophical paths.

Synchronization of the *Theology of the Body's* argument with that of *Humanae Vitae* occurs at the theological level. This requires an understanding the relationship between philosophy and theology. John Paul explains this relationship in his encyclical *Fides et Ratio* and Newman explains it in his sermon on *'Doctrine and its Development'* (OUS #15). The idea is that philosophy is at the service of theology while theology can serve philosophy by providing knowledge philosophy could not discover operating within its own rules. Saint Thomas Aquinas also gave an example of arriving at theological truth using disparate philosophical methods (that synchronize at the level of theology) in *De Veritate* and in *De Ente et Essentia* (See Part I, Chapter IV).

An example of knowledge theology provides that philosophy could not reach by itself is our contemporary understanding of personhood which derives from theological reflection on the Blessed Trinity and the Incarnation. Because of this relationship it is possible for theology to make use of all of philosophy's resources, not just those of one philosophical system in preference to all others. Theology can reach different inferences, using different philosophical tools, and synchronize all the legitimate inferences at the theological level even though their underlying philosophies resist synchronization with one another. Hence, the theological level is where the structure and method of the *Theology of the Body* and *Humanae Vitae* are synchronized.

5. How would you respond to the criticism that the theology of the body is not rigorous theology, but merely an anagogic discourse?

My response would acknowledge that the *Theology of the Body* is largely concerned with interpreting scripture in its anagogic dimension, that is, its ultimate mystical or spiritual sense. However, the *Theology of the Body* is a theological work with anagogic implications and not an anagogic discourse masquerading as rigorous theology. It is rigorous theology with a specific theological objective: to set the doctrine of *Humanae Vitae* on a more adequate anthropological foundation. The form of the *Theology of the Body* is neither mystical nor spiritual. It is theological exegesis using theological and philosophical tools and strategies commensurate with its objective. It is a concrete theological investigation of meanings scripture discloses. Among those meanings it discovers mystical and spiritual meanings.

Theological anthropology is the story of our origin, nature and destiny. One of the first points John Paul makes in the *Theology of the Body* is the need for an adequate theological anthropology (TOB 13.2). Because the *Theology of the Body* is an extended commentary on *Humanae Vitae*, this indicts *Humanae Vitae's* underlying theological anthropology as inadequate. The *Theology of the Body* searches and analyses scripture for disclosure of meanings that augment *Humanae Vitae's* anthropology. It finds in scripture the ultimate mystical or spiritual sense of the conjugal act. That does not make the *Theology of the Body* an anagogic discourse. It remains a rigorous theological treatise.

The *Theology of the Body's* philosophical methodology allows for multiple analyses of the Genesis creation narratives. These analyses investigate the personal, interior, subjective and experiential dimensions of scripture. Labeling the *Theology of the Body* an anagogic discourse is damning. It misunderstands or dismisses the value of modern philosophical approaches to the analysis of subjective experience, ignores the *Theology of the Body's* goal of proposing an adequate theological anthropology and voids its eligibility to make a theological contribution.

The *Theology of the Body* is not only a theological treatise, it is also a catechesis (TOB 133.1,1,2,4), meaning a teaching of the faith. When taught by the pope a catechesis is an exercise of the ordinary magisterium. That does not mean it is doctrine. However, this catechesis rejects previous anthropologies and proposes an anthropology in which the body and sex are integral to the *imago dei*, the image of God in man, and the prism through which all other doctrine is viewed. The stakes for this proposal are enormous. "What is at stake here is an authentically 'humanistic' meaning of the development and progress of human civilization." (TOB 129.2)

✝

www.ingramcontent.com/pod-product-compliance
Lightning Source LLC
Chambersburg PA
CBHW030937150426
42812CB00064B/2967/J